KNIGHT-CAPRON LIBRARY
LYNCHBURG COLLEGE
LYNCHBURG, VIRGINIA 24501

*Regionalism
and the Female
Imagination*

Regionalism and the Female Imagination

A Collection of Essays

Edited by

Emily Toth, PhD
Pennsylvania State University
University Park, Pennsylvania

HUMAN SCIENCES PRESS, INC.
72 FIFTH AVENUE,
NEW YORK, N.Y. 10011

Copyright © 1985 by Emily Toth
Published by Human Sciences Press, Inc.
72 Fifth Avenue, New York, New York 10011

All rights reserved. No part of this work may be reproduced or utilized in any form or by any means, electronic or mechanical, including photocopying, microfilm and recording, or by an information storage and retrieval system without permission from the publisher.

Printed in the United States of America
987654321

Library of Congress Cataloging in Publication Data
Main entry under title:

Regionalism and the female imagination.

  Bibliography: p.
  Includes index.
  1. American literature—Women authors—History and criticism—Addresses, essays, lectures.   2. Regionalism in literature—Addresses, essays, lectures.   3. United States in literature—Addresses, essays, lectures.
4. Local color in literature—Addresses, essays, lectures.
I. Toth, Emily.   II. Title.
PS152.R4   1985   810′.9′9287   83-26546
ISBN 0-89885-168-8
ISBN 0-89885-169-6 (pbk.)

CONTENTS

    Acknowledgements   7

    Introduction   9

I. NEW ENGLAND
    1. Susan Allen Toth, "The Rarest and Most Peculiar Grape": Versions of the New England Woman in Nineteenth-Century Local Color Literature   15
    2. Barbara A. Johns, Some Reflections on the Spinster in New England Literature   29

II. THE MIDWEST
    3. Paul Solyn, Lisel Mueller and the Idea of Midwestern Poetry   67

III. APPALACHIAN MOUNTAIN REGION
    4. Glenda Hobbs, Harriette Arnow's Kentucky Novels: Beyond Local Color   83
    5. Charlotte Goodman, Widening Perspectives, Narrowing Possibilities: The Trapped Woman in Edith Summers Kelley's *Weeds*   93

IV. THE SOUTH
    6. Roger Whitlow, Alice Dunbar-Nelson: New Orleans Writer   109

V. PSYCHOLOGY, RELIGION, AND REGIONALISM
    7. Cathy N. Davidson, Geography as Psychology in the Writings of

	Margaret Laurence	129
	8. Edward A. Geary, Women Regionalists of Mormon Country	139
VI.	REDISCOVERY	
	9. Bernard J. Koloski, Living, Loving, Learning: Edith Glecker's *The Rebirth of Jacob Winningstadt*	155
VII.	NEW DEFINITIONS	
	10. Arnold E. Davidson, Regions of the Mind and Margaret Gibson Gilboord's *The Butterfly Ward*	167
	11. Katherine Fishburn, Anti-American Regionalism in the Fiction of Doris Lessing	177
	Select Bibliography	189
	Notes on Contributors	197
	Index	201
	Index of Fictional Characters	205

ACKNOWLEDGEMENTS

Grateful acknowledgement is made for permissions to reprint from:

Margaret Gibson's *The Butterfly Ward* © 1976. Permission granted by Oberon Press.

Lisel Mueller's "Another Version" from *The Need to Hold Still* © 1980. Permission granted by Louisiana State University Press.

Lisel Mueller's "Highway Poems" from *The Private Life* © 1976. Permission granted by Louisiana State University Press.

Lisel Mueller's "Midwestern Poetry: Goodbye to All That" in *Voyages to the Inland Sea*, Volume I © 1971. Permission granted by the Murphy Library, University of Wisconsin-La Crosse.

Ona Siporin's *Girl on a White Gate* © 1977. Permission granted by The Private Press of Frederic Brewer (formerly Raintree Press).

Mark Vinz's "Poetry and Place: An Interview with Thomas McGrath" in *Voyages to the Inland Sea*, Volume III © 1973. Permission granted by the Murphy Library, University of Wisconsin-La Crosse.

D. Wagoner's "A Valedictory to Standard Oil of Indiana" in *Collected Poems* © 1976. Permission granted by Indiana University Press.

James Wright's "Autumn Begins in Martins Ferry Ohio" from *The Branch Will Not Break.* © 1962. Permission granted by Wesleyan University Press.

INTRODUCTION

This collection is a kind of literary archeology: finding the women buried under the label "regionalist," bringing their work to light, and giving the careful analysis it so richly deserves.

The writers of these essays are not convinced that being "regional" somehow precludes being "universal." Nor do the writers accept the belief—still too often underlying literary criticism—that the only truly significant literature is that created by or about men.

The essayists whose work is reprinted here recognize implicitly that what is most universal, most representative of "the human condition," is not necessarily war, or hunting, or the pursuit of a white whale. Rather, our most universal—most human—experiences happen at home. Our deepest emotions are associated with and expressed in the private sphere—the sphere of home, women, region.

And the work of women regionalists—letting us feel and taste the texture of real lives—may be the most universal of all.

Feminism has made all of us question the truths and assumptions we've learned in the past. One of my beliefs used to be that scholarship on women writers was of interest to only a few people, and I held that belief when I began *The Kate Chopin Newsletter* in 1975 at the University of New Orleans. I envisioned the newsletter as a small-scale publication for a coterie: those who had rediscovered Chopin. That September I moved to the University of North Dakota, and the subscription list kept growing.

New kinds of articles began appearing in my mailbox. I was reading creative syntheses of feminist criticism; I was rediscovering other regionalist writers. Without having expected it at all, I had a unique opportunity: the chance to publish genuinely original contributions to knowledge.

By the time I moved to Penn State in 1977, the newsletter had become a journal; *Regionalism and the Female Imagination.* Until publication ceased in 1979, *RATFI* provided a showcase for some of the most creative literary scholarship available, and some of the best writing. The articles reprinted here are only a sampling of those specifically concerned with regionalism and women—as writers, subjects, symbols. *RATFI* also published outstanding pieces on women's humor, on androgyny, on silences, and much more.

Although the articles published were not chosen for ethnic, racial, sexual, or regional balance, *RATFI* managed to include pieces from (or about) virtually all parts of the United States and much of Canada. It also attracted an unusually large number of male critics, as this collection demonstrates. Still, editors are limited to what they receive, and women of color are, unfortunately, slighted.

I can only hope that future writers will be analyzing and celebrating the contributions of women regionalists who are also Asian-American, Hispanic, or Black, especially since more work is now available in such collections as Dexter Fisher's *The Third Woman: Minority Women Writers of the United States* and Cherríe Moraga and Gloria Anzaldua's *This Bridge Called My Back: Writings by Radical Women of Color.*

Like the writers in those collections, the contributors to this volume share an interest in redefinition—not only of regionalism but of what constitutes significant literature and useful literary criticism. The writers pose important questions about literary neglect (as in the pieces by Charlotte Goodman, Glenda Hobbs, and Roger Whitlow). They analyze typing and stereotyping in some surprising places (Katherine Fishburn, Barbara A. Johns, and Susan Allen Toth). They bring to light lesser-known and unpublished writers (Edward A. Geary and Bernard J. Koloski), and suggest a new aesthetic for looking at women and regionalism (Arnold E. Davidson, Cathy N. Davidson, and Paul Solyn).

Most of all, the contributors to this volume are not restricted by notions of "place," for women or for regionalist writers. Theirs is a call to continue the work done here—a work of re-creation and a work of imagination.

This collection is very much a collaborative effort. I received support from the College of Liberal Arts at the University of North Dakota (Bernard O'Kelly, Dean) and the College of Liberal Arts at the Pennsylvania State University (Thomas Magner, Dean). Editorial chores for *Regionalism and the Female Imagination* and its predecessor, *The Kate Chopin Newsletter,* were shared by Eloise Arnold, Cathy N. Davidson, Glenda Hobbs, Cynthia Kinnard, Joyce Ruddel Ladenson, Mary Jane Lupton, Ellen

Elizabeth Morgan, Sharon O'Brien, Pamela (Gaudé) Parker, Peggy D. Skaggs, Vonda Kay Redman Somerville, and Marlene Springer. The contributors to this volume have also helped in compiling the Select Bibliography.

The English Department secretarial staffs at the University of New Orleans, University of North Dakota, and Pennsylvania State University aided in producing this collection. The final manuscript was typed by Margie Melton, Nancy Royer, and Dana Stuchell.

Finally, I owe particular thanks to the Human Sciences Press, especially Norma Fox, Marilyn M. Houston, Barbara Perrin, Donna Matthew, and Nancy E. Levine; to my agents, Geri Thoma and Elaine Markson; and to those who encouraged—particularly Dorothy Ginsberg Fitzgibbons, John Fitzgibbons, Elizabeth Hampsten, Susan Koppelman, Tillie Olsen, John Milton Price, Sara Ruffner, Per Seyersted, Havi Shafer and Bruce Toth.

Emily Toth
State College, Pennsylvania

I

New England

Chapter 1

"The Rarest and Most Peculiar Grape"
Versions of The New England Woman in Nineteenth-Century Local Color Literature

By Susan Allen Toth

Watching the lucidly neurotic heroine of Erica Jong's *Fear of Flying* agonize toward an independence she needs but fears and listening uncomfortably to Jong's frank criticism of men and marriage, many contemporary critics have hailed Isadora Wing as a startlingly new development among American literary characters. But the so-called "new woman" who is trying to define her personal and social position apart from man's does not simply emerge full-blown in Jong's pages. This new woman has been struggling in print for at least a century; and in post-Civil War America, observers noted her movements with much uneasiness. Puzzled gusts and vehement blasts about the "woman question" ruffled the pages, particularly, of American popular magazines from 1865 to the early twentieth century in both nonfiction articles and short stories.

Among fictional representations of this new woman, New England local color literature presents a fascinating composite of the various directions in which women seemed to be heading. Harriet Beecher Stowe, Rose Terry Cooke, Mary E. Wilkins Freeman, Sarah Orne Jewett, and Alice Brown are among the best guides to follow down these bumpy paths.

It is not surprising that New England local color writing should be an unusually rewarding source for studying the changing American woman. During this period New England still dominated the American imagination as the birthplace of the Republic, the center of intellectual life, the repository of religious and moral values. Backward glances into the American past nearly always turned East. When Harriet Beecher Stowe began the trend of New England local color fiction with *Oldtown Folks,* she prefaced the novel with her belief that a history of New England was also a history of what America was to become. Similarly, Kate Gannett Wells in an 1880 *Atlantic* article on "The Transitional American Woman" argued that "the New England woman should be taken as the largest representative of the whole country" (1).

Most New England local colorists were intensely proud of the New England woman. This pride reached a somewhat dizzy rhetorical height in Mary E. Wilson Sherwood's essay, "New England Women," in an 1878 issue of *Atlantic.* Sherwood felt that New England women were the finest America could offer. "Cold winters and short summers, a great deal of cultivation, Puritan style of clipping the tendrils, not much richness any way, and we bring to perfection the rarest, purest, most peculiar grape in all the world!" (2). Sherwood flatly claims that such women surpassed New England men: "The Puritan mothers must have been very superior to the Puritan fathers" (3). New

England women, Sherwood emphasized, were strong in will and body.

This strength is the quality New England women writers seized on as the common characteristic of their best female characters. They would agree with Sherwood that "I never saw a New England heroine beaten. I have seen her assailed by all the enemies of our race,—sickness, poverty, misfortune, disgrace, and sorrow,—and she has conquered them all" (4).

This ringing accolade evokes the figure of many a strong fictional heroine: Stowe's Grandmother Badger in *Oldtown Folks,* whose firm hand always quiets a turbulent household; Freeman's Candace in "A Village Singer," explicitly compared to Napoleon, who refuses to accept the defeat of old age and failing powers; Cooke's "Polly Mariner, Tailoress," who with sharp wits and even sharper tongue carves for herself a fiercely independent life; Brown's Lucindy in "After All," a gentle, timid old maid who, after a full life caring for a stern, ascetic father, harmlessly indulges herself in pleasures after his death. These women are all survivors who refuse to relinquish their hold on life.

Sherwood's words also echo behind our last view of Mrs. Todd in Jewett's masterpiece, *The Country of the Pointed Firs,* as that remarkably resilient woman gradually disappears from sight: "Close at hand, Mrs. Todd seemed able and warm-hearted and quite absorbed in her bustling industries, but her distant figure looked mateless and appealing, with something about it that was strangely self-possessed and mysterious" (5).

Strong as these New England women were, however, perfect and rare as they might be, they were still, as Sherwood almost unconsciously admits, a peculiar fruit of a peculiar vintage. Circumstances severely limited the choices they could make, and most New England women in this period had to confront narrowing vistas for their lives. In economically declining New England of post-Civil War days, most marriageable men had died in the recent war or had migrated westward in search of better land or jobs. "What is women's role in society?" became a pressing question when it was raised in a village in which marriage was only a distant possibility. By 1878 a writer for *Harper's* could urge women to devote themselves to charitable work simply because it was all they had left. He tried to be cheerful about the prospect: "The fact of redundancy of women, especially in Massachusetts, is one of the many blessings in disguise we are only now beginning to understand" (6). He did not report how the redundant women felt about this blessing.

His cheerfulness was not usually reflected in other articles and stories about the gradual decay of New England life. As late as 1909, Anne Warner wrote a short story for *Century* called "The New Woman and the Old" that contrasts an overeager mother and her reluctant spinster daughter as they both contemplate the only possible marriageable male in town. He is an unpromising husband, but he is all there is. The mother's complaint is an epigraph for much New England village life: "When I think of the kind of men I wouldn't have, and then of the kind you've got to have! . . . I don't know where all the young men have gone to these days, I'm sure" (7). This is the environment that nurtured Cooke, Freeman, Jewett, and Brown, and they dealt with its effects in their stories of single women.

Their responses are surprisingly various. Mary E. Wilkins Freeman specialized in portraits of neurotic single women. Sometimes these were spinsters who clung to aging marital prospects in quiet desperation, like the pathetic couple in "Two Old Lovers," who are still courting when the congenitally slow lover finally admits on his deathbed, "Maria, I'm—dyin', an'—I allers meant to—have asked you—to marry me" (8). Clarissa in "The Scent of the Roses" waits ten years for a former beau to return from the West; meanwhile she fills time by preserving rose leaves in every unused dish in the house. When he finally comes to claim her, her younger sister falls in love with him, and at the end of the tale this rejected girl begins to gather her own roses to preserve. A faint odor of decayed love, a scent of the past, hovers over these and other spinsters of Freeman's world.

Not every single woman of Freeman's wants to marry, however. Lucy, the obsessively shy heroine of "Arethusa," wants to live alone with her mother, roaming the fields freely, blooming only to herself. Although she finally gives in to marriage, she remains in full possession of her own soul; Freeman likens her husband to Alpheus, who, after winning the nymph Arethusa, "never knew that, while forever his, even in his embrace, she was forever her own" (9). In "Louisa," a strong-minded, silent, hardworking girl refuses to wed the one eligible bachelor in town, whose wealth could save her tiny family from starvation, because she does not love him. She won't sacrifice her integrity or illusions for a social institution. "Louisa had never seen anybody whom she would have preferred to Jonathan Nye. There was no other marriageable young man in the place. She had only her dreams, which she had in common with other girls" (10).

Women in Freeman's stories who eschew marriage often find other sources of emotional fulfillment. She writes compassionately about affection shared by two old sisters in stories like "A Gala Dress" or "A Mistaken Charity," and she is particularly eloquent about the love of a mother for her daughter. Although she occasionally succumbs to sentimentality on the subject of mothers, she also writes some of her best tales about the selflessness and power of this kind of love. Her daughter's plight, rather than her own, causes Mrs. Penn to rebel in the classic "The Revolt of Mother"; the mother of "A Modern Dragon" painfully changes her rough masculine dress and her spiritualist inclinations to assure her daughter's happiness; and "Old Woman Magoun," in a remarkable melodrama, actually watches in anguish as her granddaughter innocently eats deadly nightshade berries because the old woman feels this is the only way to save her from being literally sold to an unscrupulous man. Many of the strong, aggressive women who have been remarked in Freeman's fiction are mothers who must guide and protect daughters much weaker than they, and their strength raises them to heroic levels in defense of their children.

This maternal bond is one celebrated by Sarah Orne Jewett as well. Mrs. Todd and her mother have one of the closest relationships in *The Country of the Pointed Firs*. At 67, Mrs. Todd takes a child's delight in her 86-year-old mother's energy and vivacity. Sailing unannounced to her mother's island, "a quicker signal had made its way from the heart on shore to the heart on the sea. 'How do you suppose she knows it's me?' said Mrs. Todd, with a tender smile on her broad face. 'There, you never get over bein' a child long's you have a mother to go to'" (11). Both women are widows and turn naturally to each other for affection hard to find elsewhere.

In the absence of men, love between women can become uncomfortably excessive in some of Freeman's stories. Freeman features many plots in which one sister gives up a man to another or a girl sacrifices her lover for the sake of a friend. This kind of love often seems stronger than that between women and men. The plain, stolid heroine of "A Moral Exigency," for example, wins her first and only beau by taking him away from a girlhood friend. When Eunice's conscience recalls to her how one day, long ago, her friend Ada's "golden head . . . nestled on her bosom," Eunice returns her beau—who has little to say about it—to her friend. The story ends with this brief scene: "Eunice drew the golden head down on her bosom, just as she had on that old schoolday. 'Love me all you can, Ada,' she said. 'I want—something'" (12). This emotion may make some modern readers uncomfortable, but it was then an accepted part of women's lives. In *The Gentle Americans,* Helen Howe describes what became known as a "Boston marriage," the common stiuation of two single or widowed ladies who decided to share their fortunes and their lives (13). Many of the local colorists celebrate this sort of marriage in their stories.

Although Freeman became best known among this group of writers for her portraits of single women, Rose Terry Cooke is another New Englander whose fiction focuses on women who choose a single life with a deliberate sense of what they are losing—and gaining. "Polly Mariner, Tailoress" refuses to live with anyone, husband or relative.

> *I tell you what, I've made up my mind about it, 'n' it'll take a sight to change it. I a'n't one o' them complyin' and good-natered critturs that'll give up, 'n' give up, 'n' give up, till they can't call their souls their own. . . . I can't be yoked up to other folks's wants anyhow, least ways no more'n just for a spell,—say, a day or so. (14)*

In "How Celia Changed Her Mind," an old maid marries only to regret her mistake, since her husband turns out to be stingy and cruel. After he conveniently dies, she determines to keep Thanksgiving every year as an old maid's "burnt-offering," for she has concluded: "I go the hull figure with the 'postle Paul when he speaks about the unmarried, 'It is better if she so abide.'" (15).

Another spinster, in "Three of Us," reminisces about

her decision to remain single: "It is something, Jo, to know that I am not in the power of a bad, or even ill-tempered man. I can sit by my fire and know that no one will come home to fret at me,—that I shall encounter no cold looks, no sneers, no bursts of anger, no snarl of stinginess, no contempt of my opinion and advice. . . . Sensitive and fastidious as I am, I do not know whether my gain is not, to me, greater than my loss" (16).

Inextricably entangled with such praise of the single life in Cooke's stories is her implicit criticism of most married women's experiences. No other New England local colorist felt so vehemently, or observed in print so acutely, the sufferings of women—and very occasionally, men—in bad marriages. On the one hand, Cooke inveighed in print about the sanctity of marriage vows, even to the extent of arguing that "Were divorce permitted for drunkenness, insanity, poverty, incompatibility of temper, where would be self-denial, the patience, the kindly daily deeds, that marriage in its highest sense produces and fosters?" (17). On the other hand, she incorporated in story after story case histories of characters whose spirit, liveliness, and very sustenance were snuffed out by husbands who were unkind, or worse.

"Mrs. Flint's Married Experience," for example, tells about a weak-willed and soft-hearted widow who marries a grasping and merciless widower. He comes close to starving her, she finally leaves him, and the village church then descends in full force to urge her back to her duty. When she finds release in death, Cooke moralizes somewhat negatively: "Whether ever, in that far world of souls, they met again, is perhaps doubtful: let us pray not. Mrs. Flint's married experience was over in this world a hundred years ago, and in the next 'they neither marry nor are given in marriage'" (18).

Even more melodramatic is "The Ring Fetter," in which

a drunken brute of a husband literally shackles his wife's wedding ring to her hand and throws away the key, crying: "Ha, ha! going away from me!—that's a d—d good joke, a'n't it? Away from your husband! You Fool! You can't get away from me! You're mine, soul and body,—this world and the next! . . . as long as you've got on that little shiny fetter on your finger,—don't you know that?" (19). When a wedding ring has become a symbol of imprisonment, how is Cooke to end her story? Disbelieving in divorce, while presenting a rabidly emotional case for it in her story, she solves the dilemma in the only way possible. Hitty runs down to a black, rapidly moving river and leaps in. "'Look!' said she, raising her shackled arm high in air— 'I shall carry it to God!'" (20).

No other New England local colorist followed her heroines to such fierce extremes of independence, and although most of these women writers were often implicitly critical of marriage, none embodied such searing visions of it as Cooke. Instead they tended to stress the satisfactions of single life, as Cooke occasionally did, and to point to other sources of emotional fulfillment than marriage, as Freeman had. Freeman's story, "A New England Nun," remains a classic example of this theme. Louisa Ellis, the spinster who has been waiting 14 years for the return of her lover, is not to be pitied as much as her male critics have claimed. (21). When she chooses to remain unwed so that her regular and tidy routine of life will remain undisturbed, she does ignore a woman's traditional fulfillment but she does *not* have such an unpleasantly barren life in exchange: "If Louisa Ellis had sold her birthright she did not know it, the taste of the pottage was so delicious" (22).

Freeman is careful to specify, with her usual fine eye for important detail, what makes Louisa's choice appealing. Louisa's orderly house is described as a work of art: the window-panes are polished "until they shone like jewels," the bureau drawers hold "exquisitely folded contents redolent with lavender and sweet clover," the kitchen table is crowned "with a starched linen cloth whose border pattern of flowers glistened." Within this charming little house Louisa spends her time happily sewing fine seams and distilling essences from roses, peppermint, and spearmint, scents that hover over her life like mild incense. As the story ends, she is blissfully content and "fairly stepped in peace," even though her lover has chosen to marry someone else.

Alice Brown agreed with Freeman that the single life could hold its own rewards. Amelia, in "A Second Marriage," decides not to wed her former sweetheart once her husband dies, for she finds the peace, quiet, and lulling memories of the past are better company than anyone else. Her decision is symbolized by the way she sits down at her antique spinning wheel to listen to the "purring silence" of bygone days:

> *The low hum of her spinning filled the air, and she seemed to be wrapped about by an atmosphere of remoteness and memory. . . . That worldly voice, strangely clothing her own longings with form and substance, had been stilled; only the clock, rich in the tranquillity of age, ticked on, and the cat stretched herself and curled up again. (23)*

Living in the past attracted Brown's attention, and longing, again and again. In "The Way of Peace" a middle-aged lady who has spent her life peacefully tending her mother finds to her delight that when her mother dies, she herself now closely resembles the dead woman. She fixes her hair in an old-fashioned way, dons her mother's clothes, and finds deep pleasure in assuming a grandmother's role among her nieces and nephews. Lucy is transformed: "She was not herself any more; she had gone back a generation, and chosen a warmer niche" (24). There she stays, having staved off loneliness by the simple expedient of retreating into the past and assuming another life. Alice Brown does not pity her choice. She even seems to envy Dilly Joyce who, in "A Last Assembling," rejects her fiancé of many years when he returns from the city because she would have to leave her old family country home: "She had left behind her something which was very fine and beautiful; but she could not mourn. And all that morning, about the house, she sang little snatches of song, and was content. The Joyces had done their work, and she was doing hers" (25).

Such celebration of the single life reaches its muted climax in Sarah Orne Jewett's work. Among these local colorists, Jewett has received the most attention from critics of American culture and literature in recent years, and so her writing will not be discussed at length here. Most writers on Jewett agree that the world of Dunnet Landing, recorded in *The Country of the Pointed Firs,* is one of nostalgic charm, quiet appeal, warmth, and community. Yet it is also a decaying world, since its guardians are all old and no young generation waits to take their place.

Warner Berthoff characterizes the "primary myth" of Jewett's stories as "the man who went out into the world and the woman who stayed behind" (26), and he sees this myth as having tragic implications. His choice of words is interesting: "But for the women the only choice, the sacrifice required for survival, is to give up a woman's proper life and cover the default of the men, to be the guardians and preservers of a community with no other source of vitality and support" (26). *Giving up a woman's proper life*: to Berthoff this phrase evidently means that Jewett's women have no husbands to care for. Yet Jewett seems to find the lives led by Mrs. Todd, her mother Mrs. Blackett, and the narrator modeled after Jewett herself to be fruitful though single, filled with varied interests, vibrating with quiet love and concern for relatives and friends. While Jewett is no conscious proponent of the "new woman," she does contribute a series of characters who illustrate the richness of life a woman can achieve even when she must build that life alone.

From strong community leaders to shy, withdrawn spinsters; from women who cling to their mothers and sisters to women who reject sexual life entirely; from wives who do not wish to reenter marriage after widowhood has freed them, to those who endure marriage bonds as best they can, the New England nineteenth-century local color writers offer varied and surprising views of the lives of women of their time. Many of these heroines anticipate in their attitudes the independent, aggressive, even man-hating figures who have come to represent the "new woman" in twentieth-century fiction. If one has been gathering rare and peculiar grapes too long, one can even begin to see Brett Ashley emerge from a later vintage of these fields. In any case, the individual, tough-minded women the local colorists created form an all too often neglected link in the history of American women in fiction.

NOTES

1. Kate Gannett Wells, "The Transitional American Woman," *Atlantic* 46 (December 1880); 818.
2. Mary E. Wilson Sherwood, "New England Women," *Atlantic* 42 (August 1878): 230–231.
3. Sherwood, 233.
4. Sherwood, 234.
5. Sarah Orne Jewett, *The Country of the Pointed Firs* (New York: Doubleday Anchor, 1956), 159.

6. "A Glimpse at Some of Our Charities: Part II—The Employment, Education, and Protection of Women," *Harper's* 56 (March 1878): 600.
7. Anne Warner, "The New Woman and the Old," *Century* 57 (n.s.) (November 1909): 88.
8. Mary E. Wilkins Freeman, "Two Old Lovers," in *A Humble Romance and Other Stories* (New York: Harper & Bros., 1887), 36.
9. Freeman, "Arethusa," in *Understudies* (New York and London: Harper & Bros., 1901), 169.
10. Freeman, "Louisa," in *A New England Nun and Other Stories* (New York: Harper & Bros., 1891), 396.
11. Jewett, *The Country of the Pointed Firs*, 38.
12. Freeman, "A Moral Exigency," in *A Humble Romance*, 233.
13. Helen Howe, *The Gentle Americans, 1864–1960: Biography of a Breed,* New York: Harper and Row, 1965. See also Carroll Smith-Rosenberg, "The Female World of Love and Ritual: Relations between Women in Nineteenth-Century America," *Signs* 1:1 (Autumn 1975): 1–29.
14. Rose Terry Cooke, "Polly Mariner, Tailoress," in *Somebody's Neighbors* (Boston: James R. Osgood & Co., 1881), 240–241.
15. Cooke, "How Celia Changed Her Mind," in *Huckleberries Gathered from New England Hills* (Boston and New York: Houghton, Mifflin & Co., 1891), 315.
16. Cooke, "Three of Us," *Atlantic* 2 (July 1858): 143.
17. Cooke in "Women's Views of Divorce," by Mary A. Livermore, Amelia E. Barr, Rose Terry Cooke, Elizabeth Stuart Phelps, and Jennie June, *North American Review* 150 (January 1890): 123.
18. Cooke, "Mrs. Flint's Married Experience," in *Somebody's Neighbors,* 421.
19. Cooke, "The Ring Fetter: A New England Tragedy," *Atlantic* 4 (August 1859): 169.

20. Cooke, "The Ring Fetter," 170.
21. See, for example, Larzer Ziff on the story as "an example of sexual sublimation" in *The American 1890s* (New York: Viking Press, 1966), 293; and Jay Martin on its "passive sterility" in *Harvests of Change* (Englewood Cliffs, N.J.: Prentice-Hall, 1967), 150.
22. Freeman, "A New England Nun," in *A New England Nun,* 17.
23. Alice Brown, "A Second Marriage," in *Tiverton Tales* (Boston and New York: Houghton Mifflin 1899), 251, 254.
24. Brown, "The Way of Peace," in *Tiverton Tales,* 178.
25. Brown, "A Last Assembling," in *Tiverton Tales,* 174.
26. Warner Berthoff, "The Art of Jewett's *Pointed Firs,*" *New England Quarterly* (March 1959): 33.

Chapter 2

Some Reflections on the Spinster in New England Literature

By Barbara A. Johns

The resurgence of the feminist movement in the United States in recent years has brought with it a serious examination of the images of women in American fiction. This examination, by both women and men from a number of critical persuasions, has yielded such types as *the temptress, the American princess, the great mother, the new woman, the dull bovine beauty, the New England girl* (1). But no scholarship within the past 25 years has dealt comprehensively with the image of the spinster in American literature, and the subject remains curiously neglected today (2).

A study of the spinster should confront the popular notion of spinsterhood precisely on its own grounds: Does the spinster regard herself as unattractive? Is she afraid of or unresponsive to her own sexuality? Is she afraid of men and their sexuality? What choices regarding men and marriage does the society offer her? What choices does she make? Is she neurotic or repressed? Is she dour and obsessively neat? What does she do with her time and how is that time rewarded? Is there, in the fictive world she inhabits, the possibility of a healthy spinsterhood? Are there spinsters who are not simply or easily stereotyped?

A restricted study of the spinster, one that deals with a region and a time rich in women characters, would be productive in answering these questions and should be helpful in laying the foundation for a more extended study of the type in other areas of American literature. An examination of representative works of New England between 1850 and 1940—*The Scarlet Letter* (1850), *The House of the Seven Gables* (1851), *The Blithedale Romance* (1852), *Uncle Tom's Cabin: or, Life Among the Lowly* (1852), *Elsie Venner* (1851), *The Rise of Silas Lapham* (1885), *The Bostonians* (1886), *The Revolt of Mother and Other Stories* (1891), *The Country of the Pointed Firs and Other Stories* (1896), *Ethan Frome* (1911), *Mourning Becomes Electra* (1931), and *The Late George Apley* (1937)—reveals that the spinster in New England literary culture cannot be reduced to a single stereotype but exists in several modalities and that these modalities themselves constitute a statement about the time and place that is New England.

Before considering in detail the traditional New England spinster, it is worthwhile to examine an early fictional character in *The Scarlet Letter* (3) who is outside the conventional marriage norms of her time. Although there is considerable critical debate on Hester Prynne's reasons for remaining in Boston (4), it is clear that the presence of Dimmesdale there is crucial to her decision. Until her relationship with him can be resolved, she must function within Puritan society; but in order to do so, Hester, the fallen woman, ironically must assume the only role open to her. She becomes a spinster, for those problems she must deal with as a woman set apart from the community are the very things that shape a spinster's life alone. That Hester emerges as sexual, capable of making her own living, and intellectually independent during the seven years of her "spinsterhood" is not simply because she is concealing a private self behind a public face. Rather, Hawthorne's 1850 re-creation of the seventeenth-century spinster establishes several elements that will characterize one mode of New England spinsterhood for the next hundred years.

First of all, Hester's physical appearance is an index to how the woman alone must deal with her own sexuality. While at first she is marked by vital beauty and physical presence, captured in her "dark and abundant hair, so glossy that it threw off the sunshine with a gleam" (page 53), Hester's appearance gradually undergoes a "sad transformation": her "rich and luxuriant hair had either been cut off, or was so completely hidden by a cap, that not a shining lock of it ever once gushed into the sunshine" (page 163). The obvious symbol of sexuality is completely hidden, just as Hester's clothes are "of the coarsest materials and the most somber hue" (page 83); indeed, she is a picture of "studied austerity" (page 163). That Hester's appearance is not a rejection of her sexuality is clearly proved by the later forest scene with Dimmesdale. Nevertheless, her stark physical appearance illuminates one strategy by which women were apparently expected to deal with their sexuality when there was no legal or moral outlet for it in marriage, or when society regarded it as sinful (5).

Another facet of the seventeenth-century spinster's life is revealed by the social-occupational role Hester is allowed to play. Although the everyday struggles of the single woman living alone are not mentioned—"scrubbing clothes, digging a garden, chopping wood" (6)—Hester's scarlet letter is an emblem of her magnificent skill at needlework, the occupation by which she "incurred no risk of want" and that enabled her "to supply food for her thriving infant and herself" (page 81). While her sewing is her means of entering society once again (7), it is significant that the Puritans never forget Hester is an adulteress and therefore deny her work on marriage gowns. They sense that in her self-imposed solitude, in her intense privacy within a public life, and in her free life close to wilderness and sea, she has not repressed her sexuality. But even in the face of Puritan memory, Hester is allowed to take up other works of the spinster: she becomes such a "Sister of Mercy" (page 161) that the scarlet letter eventually has "the effect of the cross on a nun's bosom" (page 163). In the Puritan code of accountability, Hester does her duty to the community and thus establishes a social role for herself.

The Puritan fusion of the public and private conscience was not Hester's conscience, however, and her isolation from the community frees her to speculate and particularly to speculate on the role of women. Perhaps in response to the growing feminist movement of his own time (which had issued a far-ranging manifesto in 1848) or perhaps in response to Elizabeth Peabody's involvement in the cause, Hawthorne presents a conventional view of women who "think." It is significant that he makes the temporarily "free-thinking" Hester a woman whose impression is of "marble coldness" (page 164). Hawthorne notes that if it were not for Pearl and for the traditional role of child-raising, Hester might have acted on her dangerous thoughts about women, even to the possibility of death at the hands of a Puritan tribunal, or more horribly, to the murder of Pearl and her own suicide.

At the conclusion of the romance, Hester assures the women who seek her advice that "in Heaven's own time, a new truth would be revealed, in order to establish the whole relation between man and woman on a surer ground of mutual happiness" (page 263). The vagueness of this "new truth" and "surer ground" does not obviate what Hawthorne makes clear: the only credible spokeswoman for such a cause must show how "sacred love should make us happy, by the truest test of a life successful to such an end!" (page 263) (8). Conversely, radical thought coming from a spinster-thinker may be viewed with suspicion.

Not surprisingly, the patterns of spinsterhood that surface in *The Scarlet Letter* are not stereotypical, but they are patterns that emerge to a greater or lesser degree, in combination and in isolation, in later New England spinsters. The patterns include an appearance that is plain and somber but that does not necessarily reflect a repression of sexuality; a social role that is linked to New England "duty" and that is rewarded by the approval of society; and a solitude and freedom of thought that can contemplate the radical reordering of traditional sex roles.

Many of the spinsters in the works under consideration are indeed rather plain and unattractive, and their clothes are marked by dullness. Eunice Fairweather of Mary E. Wilkins Freeman's "A Moral Exigency" is a "tall, heavily built girl, with large, well formed feet and hands. She had a dull face, and a thick, colorless skin" (9). Inez Moore, of "A Taste of Honey" is "a little round-shouldered," and her face is of a "thick, dull-colored complexion" (page 37); in the judgment of the townspeople, she is "plain in her ways" (page 46). Louisa Britton, the main character of Freeman's "Louisa," has a face with "a clear bright look from being exposed to the moist wind" (page 57), but it is also a face that on other occasions can look "homely" or like a "closed flower" (page 62).

Another young woman, William Dean Howells's Penelope Lapham, the daughter considered to be the natural spinster of the family, has an "odd, serious face" (10). "Her large eyes, like her hair, were brown; they had the peculiar look of nearsighted eyes. . . . Her complexion was of a dark pallor" (page 36). She has little interest in clothes and, "if she had done altogether as she liked, might even have slighted dress" (page 26). Joanna Todd, Sarah Orne Jewett's reclusive spinster, is compared to her mother who "had the grim streak, and never knew what 't was to be happy" (11). Doctor Prance, a minor character in Henry James's *The Bostonians* (12), has "a sad, soft, pale face, which . . . looked as if it had been soaked, blurred, and made vague by exposure to some slow dissolvent" (page 35). She wears a "short stuff dress" under a "loose black jacket" (page 36). Miss Ophelia, the New England spinster of *Uncle Tom's Cabin* (13), is "tall, square-formed, and angular. Her face was thin, and rather sharp in its outlines; the lips compressed, like those of a person who is in the habit of making up her mind definitely on all subjects" (page 229). The plainness of these women is true for numerous other Freeman and Jewett spinsters: Elizabeth and Emily Babcock, Hetty Fifield, the Misses Bray, Aunt Cynthy Dallet, Harriet Pyne, the Dulham ladies.

Yet there is more to these New England spinsters than their homespun looks. The three young Freeman heroines, while not always pleased with their appearances, nonetheless accept them as their own; while they enjoy the attention of men, their self-worth is not determined by such attention. Eunice Fairweather likes neither her hair nor her brown cashmere dress, "but the simple facts of them ended the matter for her" (page 22). Louisa thinks that it must be the soft light that flatters her, but when she does notice her beauty, she gives "her head a little conscious turn" (page 57). Although Inez Moore "had never had anything but the very barest necessaries in the way of clothes," she lately wants to get a "bright ribbon bow to wear at the throat" (page 39). Indeed these women are "marriageable" and regard themselves as being so.

They do, however, have opinions as to what marriage should be. Eunice Fairweather's father's main concern is marrying Eunice off to a widowed minister with four children. But Eunice knows exactly what the marriage would mean: "There would be six hundred a year and a leaky parsonage for a man and woman and four children, and—nobody knows how many more" (page 25). Inez Moore has the example of her own parents' marriage, a marriage not without love but one that has nonetheless left them alone and in debt. And in spite of Louisa Britton's mother's protestations that she herself married with "common-sense," Louisa believes that her parents married for love.

Against their families' portrayal of marriage, Eunice, Inez, and Louisa hold out for romantic love, even as Hester knew there was a "consecration" with Dimmesdale far better than her passionless life with Chillingworth. But when a Freeman heroine is "confronted with principles or duties which present rival claims" (14), she invariably makes the rigorous choice, and although her one chance at love may be lost, her autonomy is preserved. Louisa Britton will simply not compromise herself: she will not look attractive for nor will she ever marry a man like Jonathan Nye, whom she despises. Eunice Fairweather, more attractive to Burr Mason than his fianceé for a quality he can't name, ironically reveals what that quality is when she gives Mason back to Ada Harris. Although Eunice at first refuses Ada's pleadings, she struggles with her conscience and finally makes the hard New England choice between duty and love. Inez Moore's choice is the same. She feels herself obliged to pay off her dead father's $600 mortgage before she can marry, and she feels obliged to pay the debt alone. She asks Willy Linfield to wait three years for her, but on the very day the debt is paid he marries another. Like Louisa and Eunice, Inez sacrifices what might appear to be conventional happiness, but she has no doubts that the higher duty had been done: "I should do it over again" (page 50).

These three women represent a special kind of spinster.

Aware of their sexuality and alive to the possibility of romance, these women regard personal integrity as an essential value that marriage ought not to violate. Spinsterhood for them is an act of moral heroism. (15).

If the Freeman women display a healthy New England "faculty" ("let a New Englander but put her mind to a problem, big or little, and the day is hers") (16), there is another set of women whose spinsterhood is a reaction to rejection rather than a clear-cut choice made on their own behalves. In the case of Irene Lapham, the reaction strengthens her in a way that marriage might never have done, but for Joanna Todd the extremity of her response kills her vitality.

As has already been noted, it was Irene's sister, Penelope, who was expected to be the spinster of the family. In addition to her plain looks, her wit (17), her interest in reading, her attendance at lectures, and her independence all mark her to the middle-class Laphams as unmarriageable. Irene, on the other hand, is the daughter to be given away. She is beautiful, not conspicuously intelligent, and perfectly willing to have her identity absorbed into marriage. She plays the courtship game by the traditional rules. Yet in spite of Irene's willingness (even eagerness) to marry, there are subtle indicators of her potential for spinsterhood. She "preferred housekeeping" (page 26), and she is more comfortable inside than outdoors.

When Howells's incredible plot of misread intentions is revealed, Irene is forced to act on her mother's "a woman grown can bear a woman's burdens" philosophy. Perhaps because of his strong, traditional views of women and marriage (18), Howells must cast Irene's reaction in the same imagery that Hawthorne used in describing Hester's "marble coldness." Irene becomes "colorless" and "immovable" (page 224) and speaks "icily" (page 225). Her face is "like a stone" (page 246), but by the next morning

Howells's imagery has shifted slightly so that she is merely "as steady and strong as a rock" (page 247). Following her preference for housekeeping, she puts her own room "to rights," then "descended upon the other rooms, which she set in order, and some of which she fiercely swept and dusted" (page 247). Irene then removes herself from the scene of her disappointment, but only temporarily. She travels to the old family home in Vermont where, like Hester Prynne, she keeps "busy helping about the house" and aiding Lapham workers "where there's sickness" (page 258). When she travels out West to an uncle's, Howells shows the reader nothing of the process of Irene's change, but she returns (in her mother's view)

> *toughened and hardened; she had lost all her babyish dependence and pliability; she was like iron; and here and there she was sharpened to a cutting edge. It had been a life and death struggle with her; she had conquered, but she had also necessarily lost much. Perhaps what she had lost was not worth keeping; but at any rate she had lost it. (page 347)*

The only real measure of what Irene lost is to see what Penelope gains. What Pen gains is a recognition of and respect for her own sexuality and emotions; but she also acquires a vacillating, helpless, dependent personality that is rewarded only when Tom Corey pays attention. Irene, now cast into traditional spinster activities, becomes self-possessed and decisive. While Howells wavers between insisting that Irene is like iron on the one hand, and holding out the possibility that she might be "rewarded" with marriage on the other, the novel has already said something else. It has shown a once immature woman who has become independent and capable through spinsterhood. Irene's "life and death struggle" is over who or what will give her self-worth. When Irene decides that a woman must determine her worth from within, she achieves the same sort of dignity as Mary E. Wilkins Freeman's decisive heroines.

Joanna Todd, Sarah Orne Jewett's reclusive spinster, responds to rejection in a manner that is ultimately suicidal. Rejected by her fiancé, Joanna lives a solitary life on the appropriately named Shellheap Island in a house she keeps "neat as a ship's cabin" (page 68). Her isolation is not the creation of personal space that Hester Prynne engages in, nor does her closeness to land and sea produce any reconciliation in her life. Rather, Joanna's grim solitude is a self-inflicted punishment, a self-abasement for what she considers the unpardonable sin of having had thoughts "so wicked toward God that I can't expect ever to be forgiven" (page 70). An old acquaintance speculates that "nowadays, if such a thing happened, she'd have gone out West to her uncle's folks or up to Massachusetts and had a change, an' come home good as new" (page 72), just as Irene Lapham had done. But Joanna does not want to be "good as new." Her "utter self-dependence, her refusal to compromise her selfhood by yielding to her friends' plea that she come ashore" (19) is a clear rejection of her own self. She has let her life be determined by one man and by an unforgiving God and to them she sacrifices her whole capacity to love and be loved. Even though there is at least one other man who still loves her, she crushes her sexuality, her social standing, her relationships, like so many broken shells.

Although the roles of the society are reversed, Joanna bears some resemblance to Hester Prynne. She carries Hester's spiritual separateness to the ultimate in physical isolation, and she takes the New England devotion to "one love" to its logical, all-or-nothing conclusion. But in the never too severe world of Sarah Orne Jewett, Joanna is allowed her social function, her "sort of a nun or hermit" role (page 61); the inhabitants of Dunnet Landing see to it that supplies are dropped on the island, and they even attend Joanna's funeral. Joanna is allowed to "fit in" as yet another modality of spinsterhood in the New England community.

The spinsters who lead active (even activist) lives are frequently the women who seem to enact the popularized version of the New England spinster. Some, like Miss Ophelia St. Clare and Doctor Mary Prance, resemble men in their toughness and efficiency: they accomplish a great deal but seem to lose an amount of human warmth and compassion in the process. Others, like Miss Tempy and Miss Birdseye, having spent themselves in causes or in "doing-for-others," possess warmth but seem literally to have given their personalities away. Each of these women lacks definition apart from what she does; they apparently have no private lives, no disappointments, no fantasies, no personal passions. They are simply asexual. But because they are not antisocial, because they do their part to sustain and preserve the social fabric, they too earn their places in a New England society that can graciously accept productive diversity.

In "Miss Tempy's Watchers," Sarah Orne Jewett chronicles the life of generous service led by the now deceased Miss Temperance Dent. On the evening before her funeral two of her best friends laud her for her cleaning, tailoring, nursing, rug-hooking, and helping at marriages. Their highest tribute—"How she did do for other folks!" (page 241)—is pronounced over her body. Although no mention is made of Miss Tempy's appearance or that she ever had a romantic interest, both of her friends acknowledge that she possessed a youthfulness that could only be attributed to a "young heart" (page 241). Miss Tempy, then, ranks among the kindly, "motherly" spinsters who are idealized by their communities even while they live.

Miss Birdseye is an elderly woman whose life has been devoted entirely to reform, especially to the Abolitionist movement. When James remarks that Miss Birdseye "belonged to any and every league that had been founded for almost any purpose whatever" (page 36), and when he observes that "since the Civil War much of her occupation was gone" (page 37), he does indeed seem to be "laughing at the entire New England heritage" (20). Insofar as Miss Birdseye represents a democratic society that James regarded as falsely conceived, it is accurate that she should be pictured as an old woman with no possessions, no peronality, no singular consciousness (21). If Boston deceives itself with its continuous series of public faces (abolitionists, socialists, mesmerists, transcendentalists, feminists) (22), Miss Birdseye is a perfect emblem of the deception, for all her philanthropy has not prevented her from "being a confused, entangled, inconsequent, discursive old woman . . . who knew less about her fellow creatures, if possible, after fifty years of humanitary zeal, than on the day she had gone into the field to testify against the iniquity of most arrangements" (page 36). In fact, she is left faceless: "the long practice of philanthropy had not given accent to her features; it had rubbed out their transitions, their meaning" (page 35). She has no personal concerns; the rumor that she might once have been romantically linked with a Hungarian is dismissed as "apocryphal" because "it was open to grave doubt that she could have entertained a sentiment so personal" (page 37).

But while James stands outside the culture and satirizes all of the Bostonians, the society within Boston regards her with affection and respect. It is the opinion of Miss Birdseye's friends that "when she should be called away the heroic age of New England life—the age of plain living and high thinking, of pure ideals and earnest effort, of moral passion and noble experiment—would effectually be closed" (page 162). Basil Ransom, the Southern outsider, cannot help but remark that her death made a difference to only three young women, but a more accurate assessment of her life is given by the more objective Doctor Prance: Miss Birdseye "was a good woman—one of the old sort" (page 343). And when James gives her "a lovely death" (page 343), he softens somewhat his earlier caustic view of her and places her in the tradition of the selfless, generous Miss Tempy.

Doctor Prance retains the bluntness of Mary E. Wilkins Freeman's women, and she is as passionless as Miss Birdseye. Her view of the sexes is intellectual and scientific: "Men and women are all the same to me. . . . I don't see any difference" (page 48). Although more private than Miss Birdseye, her privacy is not for the sake of any intimacy: "the short-haired female physician" (page 301) has "no interest beyond her researches" and is incapable of asking Basil Ransom "a personal question" (page 49). Her attitude toward the women's movement is quite negative. Ransom remarks that she was "bored with being reminded, even for the sake of her rights, that she was a woman—a detail that she was in the habit of forgetting, having as many rights as she had time for" (page 53). Doctor Prance's rights—presumably her rights to a college education, a medical practice, and an independent life—have indeed consumed her time. If Doctor Prance is intended to be the only truly liberated woman in *The Bostonians* she is successful insofar as she escapes Miss Birdseye's sentimentality and Olive Chancellor's apparent mania, but James's comment on the effect of that liberation is contained in Ransom's wish to offer the "manlike" Doctor Prance a cigar. Yet she escapes being categorized as simply as Ransom would wish, because she can turn her wry wit on him as easily as on the reformers and because the composite portrait of her is of an intelligent, unemotional, independent woman who is detached from spurious causes (23). Although clearly having no romantic desires and no life apart from her profession, Doctor Prance nonetheless achieves an identity that will not be absorbed into anyone else's. She wears her spinsterhood comfortably.

Ophelia St. Clare is another "practical, business-like" (page 243) New England spinster. Ophelia knits, sews, cooks, does "housekeeping in all its branches" (page 230). All her movements are "sharp, decided, and energetic," and she is a "living impersonation of order, method, and exactness" (page 229). Ophelia abhors "shiftlessness" and favors conscientiousness; she is "the absolute bond-slave of the *'ought'*" (page 230). She withdraws from her own family's arguments but when troubles besiege others, she relates the story with "great strength of detail . . . enlarging on its most shocking particulars" (II, page 6).

Ophelia's interest in other people's lives is indicative of her having little or no life of her own at age 45. Still considered one of "the children" (page 227) by her parents, she has no love life, no apparent romantic desires, no sexual attractiveness. But Ophelia clearly cares for Augustine St. Clare, whom she had helped to raise, "her heart having a warm side to it," and "although she regards him as something of a heathen, "yet she loved him, laughed at his jokes, and forbore with his feelings" (page 231).

In turn, Ophelia is loved by St. Clare, who can see more in her than Basil Ransom could ever appreciate in the New England women he met. Ophelia is also well regarded by the society in which she lives. Her decision to go South is discussed all over her village, but the discussion, in spite of Stowe's comic treatment, is not simply gossip. Ophelia has a place of respect in the society, as the two weeks of farewell teas given by "all her friends and neighbors" (page 228) attest. Miss Ophelia has her place in New England society.

A noteworthy aspect of the spinsters reviewed thus far is their connection with the outdoors, with things natural. Not one is housebound, and only Ophelia is obsessed with the law of order and neatness. Inez Moore and Louisa Britton farm: they plant potatoes, rake hay, take produce to market. Miss Tempy, too, is close to the earth, and though she has only one old quince tree, "she'd go out in the spring and tend to it, and look at it so pleasant, and kind of expect the old thorny thing into bloomin'" (page 241). Doctor Prance makes "constant expeditions to fish and botanise" (page 323) while visiting Cape Cod, and the venerable Miss Birdseye's last wish is to be buried "in sight of the pretty sea-view she loved to gaze at" (page 343). These spinsters, like Hester, remain close to earth and sea, and they radiate in that respect an emotional health, a sensitivity to the rhythms of life that prevents their being regarded as repressed or sick.

It is the opposite tendency, a penchant for order, a preference for the indoors, and a solitude akin to a religious retreat that makes the spinsters who are more tolerated than respected in New England society. The clearest example of such a character is Louisa Ellis of Mary E. Wilkins Freeman's "A New England Nun."

What happens to Louisa in the 14 years of waiting for her fiancé's return is that in spite of retaining her beauty, she becomes the "old maid" spinster, the woman whose energy is not channeled into village service or reform movements or medicine, but into a neurotic rage for order. Louisa has "the enthusiasm of an artist over the mere order and cleanliness of her solitary home" (page 89), and like the artist, she selects her materials carefully. She wears three aprons at once: one for tea, one for sewing, one for company. She cannot remember that "ever in her life she had mislaid" any of her sewing equipment (page 79); when she throws currant stems into the hen coop, she "looked sharply at the grass beside the step to see if any had fallen there" (page 80); she eats "in a delicate, pecking way" (page 81); she inspects the carpet after Joe leaves to see how much dust he has tracked in; she compulsively puts books back in their original arrangement after Joe has misplaced them.

What Louisa fears is disturbance, especially the disturbance of men, and therefore of passion and of sex:

> *"She had visions, so startling that she half repudiated them as indelicate, of coarse masculine belongings strewn about in endless litter; of dust and disorder arising necessarily from a coarse maxculine presence in the midst of all this delicate harmony." (page 89).*

Her worry over the endurance of purity is perfectly captured in her fears over her dog, Caesar. Joe has already set Louisa's canary into a wild commotion merely by entering the room; now that he intends to release a "killer dog." Louisa fuses Joe, the canary, and the dog into one large image of "disorder and confusion in lieu of sweet peace and harmony"; she "thought of her approaching marriage and trembled" (page 91). The sexual fear is unmistakable.

For Louisa, whose days and life are repeatedly described as "peaceful," "serene," "smooth," and "calm," the canceled marriage is a great blessing. As the title of the story indicates, she has become a New England nun, a spinster who "gazed ahead through a long reach of future days strung together like pearls in a rosary, every one like the others, and all smooth and flawless and innocent, and her heart went up in thankfulness" (page 97). At the end, she sits in her house "prayerfully numbering her days, like an uncloistered nun" (page 97). This placid ending, wherein Louisa Ellis has no sense of having sold her birthright, can be read as life-affirming in that Louisa does apparently choose for herself what will give her satisfaction (see Susan

Allen Toth, "'The Rarest and Most Peculiar Grape'"; *this volume*). But the all-pervading image of death seems to govern the scene and set its conclusive tone (24), and this image is important, for it is an element that will find its fruition in the more seriously disturbed spinsters. Louisa Ellis—neat, calm, virginal—is harmless, useless, and dying a natural death.

Another distinct mode of spinsterhood includes those women whose affections are apparently expressed outside of or apart from the conventional norms. To those beyond the immediate circle of their emotional lives, these women seem to be marked by coldness. This attitude is often, however, a mask for a deep love that must protect itself from the misinterpretation and menacing power of an unsympathetic society. In some cases, these spinsters become victims of their own false perceptions of society; in others, they are themselves powerless to act on a social order that itself is falsely conceived. With one exception, these women are reluctant to take up the social role offered the New England spinsters previously discussed. They tend to remain within their homes, apart from nature or gardens or beauty, and they are obsessively concerned with the privacy of those homes.

Hepzibah Pyncheon of *The House of the Seven Gables* (25) is an aristocratic spinster who must open a cent-shop in order to survive. This is profoundly disturbing as she has spent the past 25 years of her life secluded within the house. Hepzibah not only does not possess the sewing talents that a spinster could employ in making money, but she also lacks the attitudes necessary to be a successful schoolteacher, for "the love of children had never been quickened in Hepzibah's heart" (page 39). She has an unfortunate nearsighted scowl that in 60 years has made people believe that she is "an ill-tempered old maid" (page 34), a judgement that she believes about herself. She does not enjoy any of the delights of nature or of ordinary living. She has "no taste nor spirits for the ladylike employment of cultivating flowers, and . . . would hardly have come forth, under the speck of open sky, to weed and hoe, among the fraternity of beans and squashes" (page 87). Neither does Hepzibah have any "natural turn for cookery" (page 99). Old maid that she is, Hepzibah does not, however, have Louisa Ellis's or Irene Lapham's compulsion to neatness. The house is dusty and dark, and the aristocratic Hepzibah is rather proud that she has no talent for homemaking.

Yet Hepzibah does have a lover: her family in the person of her brother Clifford. Early in the romance, Hepzibah looks at a portrait of the "strong passion of her life" (page 31):

> *Can it have been an early lover of Miss Hepzibah? No; she never had a lover—poor thing, how could she?— nor ever knew, by her own experience, what love technically means. And yet, her undying faith and trust, her fresh remembrance, and continual devotedness towards the original of that miniature, have been the only substance for her heart to feed upon. (page 32)*

When Clifford returns home, Hepzibah does everything for him, with a devotion more intense than the dutiful and solicitous generosity expected in the New England tradition of ministering sisters. As she attempts to cook a meal for him, to read to him in her croaking voice, to sing for him while accompanying herself on the harpsichord, she is channeling her pride in the Pyncheon name, her outrage at the injustices done Clifford, and her mistrust of Salem into the only form that seems safe from the greed of her cousin Jaffrey and the democracy of the streets. Romantic and worshipful love is the only way Hepzibah can act on her universe, since she cannot match the public power of the Judge nor can she endure what she sees as the vulgarity of the Yankee public. That this love for her brother, confined as it is to the privacy of her home, is so pathetically inward, so trapped, indeed so without reciprocation, is a measure of the helplessness of Hepzibah's branch of the Pyncheons.

After trying to improve her appearance by "putting ribbons on her turban" (page 136), she finally, sadly, surrenders all her attempts at being the medium of Clifford's happiness. For Hepzibah this is the supreme sacrifice, for making him happy "would have rewarded her for all the past, by a joy with no bright tints, indeed, but deep and true, and worth a thousand gayer ecstacies" (page 136). But any "deep and true tints" and "gayer ecstacies" have long since been subsumed under a complex rubric of sisterly devotion, and even Phoebe's and Holgrave's affection cannot obviate what Holgrave knows to be true: "Miss Hepzibah, by secluding herself from society, has lost all true relation with it, and is in fact dead" (page 216).

This death imagery, so reminiscent of Joanna Todd and Louisa Ellis, helps to locate the social significance of Hepzibah. The brother and sister almost constitute a perverse married couple, the logical end of a perversely founded family, and New England society reacts accordingly when it does not come to their aid. It is Hepzibah's tragedy that she is not Miss Tempy or Doctor Prance or Miss Birdseye; in her misplaced isolation, her inwardness, her love that cannot leave the bounds of family, she provides an image of a failed aristocracy that is more striking in its human pathos than the symbol of the abandoned house of the seven gables. Hepzibah's spinsterhood is a parable of misspent pride at the cost of her own life made sadly colorless.

Olive Chancellor of *The Bostonians* is the reformer for women that Hester Prynne might have wanted, but she is not the long-married, faithful angel of change. Physically, she is a "signal old maid" (page 29). The narrator remarks, "There are women who are unmarried by accident, and others who are unmarried by option; but Olive Chancellor was unmarried by every implication of her being" (page 29). She is so essentially a spinster that Basil Ransom thinks of her as old. He sees her "white skin . . . drawn tightly across her face" and her eyes with their "glitter of green ice"; he notes that "she had absolutely no figure, and presented a certain appearance of feeling cold" (page 29). Her "smooth, colourless hair" is carefully combed, and she wears the usual "plain dark dress" (page 22). Indeed, Olive "loathed and despised" (page 101) the world of fashion.

Olive is similar to Joanna Todd in having a certain grim aspect to her character. She is a person who "took things hard," "a woman without laughter" (page 29). Like Hepzibah, she remains inside a great deal. Ransom feels that he has never been "in the presence of so much organized privacy or so many objects that spoke of habits and tastes" (page 27). Her house is "thoroughly well regulated," and she is "passionately clean" (page 157). Olive "had never favoured the custom of running in and out" (page 157), and even when she herself entertains, it is at preappointed hours. Her ecstatic visions are of "still winter evenings under the lamp, with falling snow outside and tea on a little table" (page 84). Like Joanna and Louisa, she also seems attracted to death, although her preference is not for their slow deaths, but to be "a martyr and die for something" (page 24). The "something" is the women's movement, and she imagines herself joined with other women, "asking no better fate than to die for it" (page 45).

The affection in Olive's life is given to Verena Tarrant. Their first private meeting is charged with language that will characterize their whole relationship: a "language of love" (26). The narrator reveals that "from this first interview she [Verena] felt that she was seized" (page 78), and she remembers that it was Olive's glance "that was the beginning; it was with this quick survey, omitting nothing, that Olive took possession of her" (page 78). How intensely Olive wishes to take possession is indicated by her demanding of Verena, "Promise me not to marry!" (page 124). Even when she later casts the promise in terms of a feminist priesthood, it is clear that Olive's affection has a more personal sexual politics at its roots (27). Many critics have interpreted this sexual politics and Olive's real cause to be not feminism but Verena Tarrant herself, not a public social movement but a private lesbian passion (28).

But Olive's desire for Verena should not be seen as "perverse," "unnatural," or "evil" simply because it is woman-centered, nor because Olive herself may not understand the depths of her own emotion, nor because Olive may have to justify her passion even to herself by making it part of a political cause. Indeed, as Judith Fetterly has argued, Olive's powerlessness in the face of Ransom's traditional male power can be seen as the true source of her morbidity, isolation, and rigidity, and her apparent man-hating can be read as simply a response to the world as she sees it. (29). It is Olive's tragedy that her love for Verena is doomed on a cultural battlefield where women have no real power and where she cannot hope to win.

When Olive's "intense personal oneliness" (30) and "homeless ego" (31) find no salvation in Verena, Olive is granted some measure of self-realization, something never achieved by Ransom, who persists in his own delusions to the end. The battle between Olive and Ransom at the Cape, with Olive entrenched in her "cottage-fortress" (page 335), is effectually concluded when Olive for the first time admits to herself that Verena does not love her. In an agonizing scene, Olive relives every moment of her two years with Verena, and when Verena returns to the cottage, they sit alone in a darkened parlor, where "it was a kind of shame" (page 353). The Olive who in private moments could show "a tone of softness and sympathy, a gentle dignity, a serenity of wisdom" (page 127), is now clearly revealed in the vulnerability and loneliness common to all unrequited lovers. The iciness, the hardness, the sadness that Olive displays to the other Bostonians, the spinsterhood that is "in every implication of her being" are not signals of a perversity in Olive. They are simply the armor with which she seeks to protect her own heart and soul.

The signs of Lavinia Mannon's spinsterhood are evident throughout *Mourning Becomes Electra* (32), although many of those traits also can be assigned to her compelling Electra complex. Her movements are indeed like her father's, but her appearance is the spinster's: "her body is thin, flat-breasted and angular and its unattractiveness is accentuated by her plain, black dress" (page 23). Although Lavinia looks like her mother, especially in their beautiful "peculiar shade of copper-gold hair" (page 23), her behavior is the exact opposite of Christine's love of nature and life. Christine remains outside in the garden while Lavinia often spends an entire day in her bedroom. Christine warns Vinnie against any interest in Spring, for it would not become a "Puritan maiden" (page 72). Christine calls the house a "tomb" but notes that Lavinia likes it because it "suits your temperament" (pages 31–32).

When Lavinia finally recognizes her incestuousness as the root of her responses to her mother, father, brother, Adam Brant, and Peter Niles, her reaction is immediate and not unlike those of other spinsters discussed previously. She "grimly" orders the gardener to throw out all the flowers, and "with frozen eyes" (page 246) she determines to live alone in the Mannon house. "'I'll never go out or see anyone! I'll have the shutters nailed closed so no sunlight can ever get in. I'll live alone with the dead, and keep their secrets, and let them hound me, until the curse is paid out and the last Mannon is let die!" (page 256). Lavinia's reaction bears a close resemblance to the "religious" behavior of other New England spinsters. But hers is not the public martyrdom of Olive Chancellor nor the serene contemplation of the New England nun. Lavinia's spinsterhood is closer to Joanna Todd's, but it lacks even her slight hope that an "unpardonable sin" can be pardoned through penance.

It is ironic that Lavinia is closest to Hester Prynne in acting on her sexuality, yet unlike Hester, she cannot ever reconcile nature and law and guilt. Instead, out of her recognition that sexual desire has motivated her acts of "justice," she chooses the most repressive form of spinsterhood in order to punish herself. She embraces a living suicide with no hope that actual death will bring her regeneration or peace. In the New England tradition, the repressed spinster, the isolated woman who is so out of touch with her society that she fights its very foundations, is condemned to a living death.

To the spinsters reviewed thus far can be added those women who bear many of the characteristics of spinsterhood but who turn up, at the conclusions of the novels in which they appear, as married women. Although they have been nearly bodiless, sickly, and passionless, they are chosen by men; they are the "fair-haired maidens" of American literature who represent conventionality, traditional sex-roles, passivity (33). When the creators of these spinsters marry them off, they are saying as much about the passion within American marriages as they are about spinsterhood.

Priscilla, of Hawthorne's *The Blithedale Romance* (34), is a "slim and unsubstantial girl" (page 26). On her entrance to Blithedale, she is "dressed in a poor but decent gown, made high in the neck, and without any regard to fashion or smartness.... her face was of a wan, almost sickly hue" (page 27). Although Priscilla is inept at nearly all domestic activities, she is an accomplished seamstress and is admired for her "fine needlework" (page 51). Her immediate relation to the unhealthy spinsters discussed previously is reinforced by her unfamiliarity with nature, by her having "been bred up, no doubt, in some close nook" (page 35), "in a small, close room" (page 34), where "a little parallelogram of sky" (page 35) would have been all she'd known of nature.

Priscilla's psychic distance from the vitality of land and sea is evident in her disquietude during storms, her inability to compete in an outdoor footrace beause she has grown up without exercise, and in her blossoming—"'She is as lovely as a flower!" (page 169)—in the city rather than in the country. Coverdale notes that Priscilla "had gone far enough in her teens to be, at least, on the outer limits of girlhood" (page 50), but she remains an adolescent. She may develop some "wildness" (page 59) as she goes a-Maying, clambers up on hay wagons, and rides oxen, but her vitality is that of a child, not a woman (35). In fact, the nature imagery surrounding her is invariably in terms of airiness or passivity: she is a "shadowy snow-maiden" (page 33); she "melted in quietly" (page 35); she is "a butterfly, at play in a flickering bit of sunshine" (page 74).

If Priscilla does not seem to inhabit a woman's body, neither does she seem to inhabit a woman's psyche. There is simply no passion or urge in her life that might be considered an expression of her own identity or autonomy. Where other spinsters have loved *something* (their careers or their causes, if not other women or men), Priscilla can only say of herself, "I am blown about like a leaf. I never have any free-will" (page 171). She is indeed a medium, a veiled lady, transparent as sunshine or wine (36), a woman whose only affection is a "silent sympathy . . . unalloyed with criticism" (pages 78–79), and whose effect on men is to convince them of their "right to all the worship that is voluntarily tendered" (page 79).

Zenobia is perfectly correct when she contemptuously exclaims of Priscilla: "She is the type of womanhood, such as man has spent centuries in making it. He is never content, unless he can degrade himself by stooping towards what he loves" (page 122). When Hollingsworth marries Priscilla and Coverdale admits his love for her, both admit that they prefer "love without passion, art without energy, woman without body" (37). They do indeed stoop toward their idealized version of true womanhood, but their posture is as ironic and as ultimately destructive for Priscilla as it is for themselves. For in becoming whatever men want her to be, even to being a sexless, passionless, disembodied spinster disguised to herself as a married woman, Priscilla has chosen nothing for herself. All the "romance" at Blithedale—including Priscilla's veiled spinsterhood—is, finally, tragic.

Helen Darley of Oliver Wendell Holmes's *Elsie Venner* (38) is not a tragic character, but she is as vacuous as Priscilla and as rewarded in the end. Helen represents what Louisa Britton or Eunice Fairweather might have become if they had not possessed such a strong sense of their own self-worth. Left to make her own living after her clergyman-father's death, the meek, sweet, apple, blue-eyed Helen becomes a schoolteacher. "Dependent, frail, sensitive, and conscientious," Helen is an "overworked woman" who suffers from "many varieties of headache," neuralgia, backaches, fits of depression, and "paroxysms" (page 69). She is particularly subject to Elsie Venner's strange powers; insofar as Elsie is an Eve-like temptress (39), Helen is in marked contrast to her, as Priscilla stands opposed to Zenobia.

While Helen seems to have more endurance than Priscilla (in spite of her constant exhaustion), she is like her in timidity. She never speaks to the principal about her unfair wages; in fact, she doesn't speak up to men at all and thus becomes, again like Priscilla, an idealized, nonthreatening, worshipful, bodiless woman. Bernard Langdon regrets that she might never be told what an "angel" (page 230) she is on earth. He writes to a friend: "Why does not somebody come and carry off this noble woman, waiting here all ready to make a man happy? . . . Do you know the pathos there is in the eyes of unsought women oppressed with the burden of an inner life unshared?" (page 230). Of course, this inner life can only be shared by a man, and when the older Dudley Venner offers himself in marriage, the "inner life" seems to be exactly what he wants.

But if one cannot sense Helen's "body through her clothes" (40), Helen herself is not even sure she can sense her own mind: she is "surprised" and "bewildered"; she calls herself "a poor faded flower, not worth the gathering of such a one as you" (page 467); she can answer Venner's proposal with only a faltering "What can I say?" (page 469). Helen is a typical sentimental heroine, but she also seems to be something more: a woman without body or mind who simply acquiesces to life. Dudley Venner's discovery is yet to come: he has married (as has Hollingsworth) yet another kind of New England spinster. Should he seek to touch her, he'll find nothing there.

When Basil Ransom called Olive Chancellor "unmarried by every implication of her being," he was not altogether accurate, for Olive, as we have seen, did have some passion in her life. The spinsters who do meet Ransom's description are those who seem to have been born to the part, who are spinsters *ab ova,* and who match every stereotype of the spinster as it exists in the popular imagination. These women are not the passive Priscillas or Helen Darleys; they do have feelings, but their emotional energy is directed toward protecting themselves. Consistent with the patterns already established, they keep men at a distance by their coldness, their sickliness, their well-ordered routines, their sanctuary-like homes. They are not asexual; they are sexually frigid. Their barriers are civilized but secure. But oddly enough, these women are not single at all. They are New England's married spinsters. They are like a character in a recent American novel who merely endures marriage, who tells her granddaughter: "There are certain duties in a marriage. . . . There are certain things one has to go through with because the man needs them, you see" (41).

Unlike Hester Prynne, Catharine Apley of *The Late George Apley* (42) would not think of rejecting a marriage because it might be without love or passion. Rejection does not occur to her (as it clearly did to the Freeman women) because Catharine's aristocratic social class demands that its daughters marry. Neither would Brahmin Boston allow her the placid, uncommitted life of a Louisa Ellis. Yet Catharine does withdraw into her own well-ordered, self-sufficient world once she has suffered through the painful necessities of marriage ceremony and wedding night.

Catharine has previously demonstrated her propensity for gathering things rather than people, as with her large butter knife collection. On their honeymoon she spends her time avoiding George: she writes thank-you notes, crochets bedspread squares, and invites her parents to join them, for "two weeks alone is rather a long time" (page 130). When George writes that "Catharine says we never really knew each other until we came here, and I am inclined to agree" (page 130), he is speaking prophetically, for he will never know her any better than on his honeymoon. She fills up the evenings of their marriage with sewing, making sure that pen and ink are ready so that George can fill up his nights with writing speeches to be delivered on still other evenings. She does retain some link with nature at George's summer camp, but even that connection is twisted when she civilizes the camp with rules and regulations. Catharine will have nothing to do with animals; she will not allow the children to have pet dogs nor will she share George's interest in bird-watching. This aversion is similar to Louisa Ellis's sexual fear of the "disturbance" of dogs and canaries. Louisa's compulsion to order and neatness is also evident in Catharine, who is always busy dusting, arranging things, or redecorating a bedroom or parlor.

When George writes to his son, "I can frankly say that sex has not played a dominant part in my own life" (page 294), he is in fact acknowledging all that Catharine has done to avoid it. Catharine is relieved when she is ignored, when George can displace her with other women. She surrenders him to Clara Goodrich (hoping that George can sublimate his desires in shared bird-watching), and even George's mother writes that Clara "gives you much that dear Catharine does not, and that is why Catharine is generous enough to love her too" (page 202). Perhaps that is also why, when Catharine greets Mary Monahan, "she took her hand with most unusual impulsiveness and said: 'I am so glad that you are looking after George'" (page 320). But, of course, George's social class and Puritan background will not allow him satisfaction outside marriage, and no matter what his wife or mother or Clara say, he is expected to look and not touch. George is a victim of Catharine's spinsterhood.

Catharine's rubber tree plant is the strongest symbol of her frigidity. She has clung to the plant since she was six years old, tending it herself, even carrying it with her into her marriage. When Catharine insists that the conservatory roof be enlarged to accommodate the plant, "the oldest in New England" (page 284), whose branches she cannot bear to cut back, she is as much as saying that nothing must penetrate her or it. George's comment that "in our day a girl was brought up to understand that her first duty was to find a suitable husband and to establish a home of her own" (page 295) is an epitaph for his own marriage. Catharine has done her "duty" and has indeed established a home entirely her own. Unfortunately, it is as fortress-like and as barricaded as Olive Chancellor's or Lavinia Mannon's. It is a spinster's home.

The ultimate in cold, icy, married spinsterhood is Zeena Frome, who inverts every positive quality of both spinsterhood and marriage in *Ethan Frome* (43). Zeena is "tall and angular," flat-chested, with a "puckered throat" and "hollows and prominences in her high-boned face" (page 27). Her hair consists only of "thin strands," and she dresses herself in a "calico wrapper and knitted shawl" (page 31). Her face is frequently "drawn and bloodless," and at 35, she is "already an old woman" (page 32). There is no love or sexual passion in her life; she apparently feels none for Ethan nor seems ever to have, and there is no indication that she has provided him with any kind of sexual satisfaction.

When Ethan becomes infatuated with Mattie Silver, Zeena does everything possible to destroy any enjoyment either Mattie or Ethan may find in each other. She complains incessantly—about her health, about the quality of her care and Mattie's help, about how Ethan tracks snow into the kitchen. Loving household order, the indoors, and the security of possessions, she reacts violently to the accident in which one of her prized wedding presents, a red pickle dish, is broken while being used for a dinner Mattie had prepared for Ethan. Whether she recognizes the possible intimacy of their dinner or the sexual significance of the broken dish (unused since their marriage) (45), her reaction is compulsive and violent: "You've taken from me the one thing I cared for most of all!" (page 63). When Ethan sees her extreme reaction, he finally understands that "the one pleasure left her was to inflict pain on him" (page 64). Then when his attempted marriage/suicide with Mattie fails, the triumphant Zeena is left to care for both of them, the icy victor in a battle for possession. Zeena is incapable of human love; she imposes the horrible isolation of her own Shellheap Island on everyone she meets in her grotesque married spinsterhood.

If one of the failures of the New England writers is that none has created the viable spokeswoman for the women's movement that Hawthorne suggested in 1850, one of their triumphs is that they have not reduced their spinster characters to a single stereotype. These women cannot be generalized as sexless fussbudgets or gossips, busybodies or do-gooders. Their attitudes about themselves are remarkably diverse, as are the roles they play in society. Whether nurses, seamstresses, physicians, abolitionists, farmers, or schoolteachers, some are self-effacing and helpless, and some are independent and self-assertive. There are those who are spinsters for a lifetime and others who embrace the role only for a moment. There are old spinsters and young, rich and poor. There are spinsters born to the part, others who are conditioned to it, and still others who choose it. The reasons behind their choices are as different as the women themselves.

This remarkable variety of New England spinsters is perhaps owing to the equally remarkable tolerance of New England society, at least as those spinsters and that society are revealed in literature. That tolerance gladly admits almost all behavior. What is not permitted is, in Hawthorne's terms, the violation of the truth of the human heart. The ultimate integrity of the person, a value operative in Hawthorne's nineteenth-century version of the Puritan community, exists into the fiction and drama of the middle twentieth century. The socially unaccepted, isolated, unproductive spinsters are those who have in some fashion laid siege to the sanctity of another person. The Zeenas, the Lavinias are left to themselves. The spinsters whose graves are honored in the end are those women who created lives for themselves and, in whatever halting way, shared it with their communities.*

NOTES

1. See Judith Fryer, *The Faces of Eve: Women in the Nineteenth Century American Novel* (New York: Oxford University Press, 1976); Mary Allen, *The Necessary Blankness: Women in Major American Fiction of the Sixties* (Urbana: University of Illinois Press, 1976); Paul John Eakin, *The New England Girl: Cultural Ideals in Hawthorne, Stowe, Howells and James* (Athens: University of Georgia Press, 1976).
2. The only full-length study of the spinster remains Dorothy Yost Deegan's *The Stereotype of the Single Woman in American Novels* (New York: King's Crown Press, 1951). While Deegan cannot be faulted for having done her work 25 years too soon, her method simply does not meet current needs.
3. Nathaniel Hawthorne, *The Scarlet Letter*, vol. I of The Centenary Edition of the Works of Nathaniel Hawthorne (Columbus, OH: Ohio State University

---

*I would like to thank Professor Seymour L Gross and the members of the seminar in New England Literary Culture, 1850–1950, at the University of Detroit for their assistance in the preparation of this paper.

Press, 1962); all page references will be to this edition.

4. See, for example, Seymour L. Gross, "'Solitude, and Love, and Anguish': The Tragic Design of *The Scarlet Letter*," and Roy R. Male, "Transformations: Hester and Arthur," in *The Scarlet Letter,* ed. Sculley Bradley et al. (New York: Norton, 1961), 359–67, 331–41.
5. For an interesting discussion of women's dress in the Shaker communities, dress quite similar to Hester's, see Judith Fryer, "American Eves in American Edens," *American Scholar* 44 (Winter 1974–75): 83.
6. Ernest Earnest, *The American Eve in Fact and Fiction, 1775–1914* (Urbana: University of Illinois Press, 1974), 63.
7. Roy R. Male, "Transformations," 333.
8. See Nina Baym, "Hawthorne's Women: The Tyranny of Social Myths," *Centennial Review* 15 (1971): 250–72.
9. Mary E. Wilkins Freeman, *The Revolt of Mother and Other Stories* (Old Westbury: The Feminist Press, 1974): "A Moral Exigency," 19–35; "A Taste of Honey," 36–52; "Louisa," 53–78; "A New England Nun," 116–39; all page references to this edition.
10. William Dean Howells, *The Rise of Silas Lapham,* vol. 12 of A Selected Edition of W. D. Howells (Bloomington: Indiana University Press, 1971), 36; all page references to this edition.
11. Sarah Orne Jewett, *The Country of the Pointed Firs and Other Stories,* ed. Willa Cather (Garden City: Doubleday, 1956), 68; "The Country of the Pointed Firs," 13–160; "Miss Tempy's Watchers," 233–43. All page references to this edition.
12. Henry James, *The Bostonians* (London: John Lehmann, 1952); all page references to this edition.
13. Harriet Beecher Stowe, *Uncle Tom's Cabin*: *or, Life*

Among the Lowly. Charles E. Merrill Standard Editions (Columbus, OH: Charles E. Merrill Publishing Co., 1969); all page references to this edition.

14. Austin Warren, *The New England Conscience* (Ann Arbor, MI: The University of Michigan Press, 1966), 162.
15. My reading of these three stories significantly disagrees with Alice Glarden Brand's recent article, "Mary Wilkins Freeman: Misanthropy as Propaganda," *New England Quarterly* 50 (March 1977): 83–100, in which she argues: "Spinsterhood was considered a social anomaly to be disparaged and avoided at all costs. Freeman resented her long, single status and, in her writings, was obsessed with barren courtships; she did not recommend spinsterhood as a life style, but rather commiserated with it."
16. Babette Mary Levy, "Mutations in New England Local Color," *New England Quarterly* 19 (September 1946): 340.
17. See Alfred Habegger, "Nineteenth-Century American Humor: Easygoing Males, Anxious Ladies, and Penelope Lapham," *PMLA* 91 (October 1976): 884–99.
18. Earnest, 146–54.
19. Perry Westbrook, *Acres of Flint: Writers of Rural New England, 1870–1900* (Washington, D.C.: Scarecrow Press, 1951), 72.
20. Donald David Stone, *Novelists in a Changing World: Meredith, James, and the Transformation of English Fiction in the 1880's* (Cambridge, MA: Harvard University Press, 1972), 269.
21. See Robert Emmet Long, "Transformations: *The Blithedale Romance* to Howells and James," *American Literature* 47 (January 1976): 552–71.
22. See Robert Emmet Long, "The Society and the

Masks: *The Blithedale Romance* and *The Bostonians*," *Nineteenth Century Fiction*, 19 (September 1964): 105–22.

23. See Cynthia Griffin Wolff, "Mirror for Men: Stereotypes of Women in Literature," *Massachusetts Review* 13 (Winter-Spring 1972): 205–18, for her discussion of the stereotype of the liberated woman.

24. See David Hirsch, "Subdued Meaning in 'A New England Nun,'" *Studies in Short Fiction* 2 (1965): 124–36.

25. Nathaniel Hawthorne, *The House of the Seven Gables*, vol. 2 of The Centenary Edition of the Works of Nathaniel Hawthorne (Columbus, OH: Ohio State University Press, 1965); all page references to this edition.

26. Mildred E. Hartsock, "Henry James and the Cities of the Plain," *Modern Language Quarterly* 29 (1968): 303. Hartsock joins other critics (mostly male) in reading the novel as a story of lesbian love or "inversion"; see note 28.

27. Paul John Eakin, "Margaret Fuller, Hawthorne, James, and Sexual Politics," *South Atlantic Quarterly*, 75 (Summer 1976): 323–38.

28. For representative discussions of Olive's relationship with Verena, see Edmund Wilson, "The Ambiguity of Henry James," in *The Question of Henry James: A Collection of Critical Essays*, ed. F. W. Dupee (New York: Henry Holt and Co., 1945), 160–90; William McMurray, "Pragmatic Realism in *The Bostonians*," in *Henry James: Modern Judgements*, ed. Tony Tanner (London: Macmillan & Co., 1968), 160–65; Charles Samuels, *The Ambiguity of Henry James* (Urbana, IL: University of Illinois Press, 1971), 91–107; Robert McLean, "*The Bostonians*: New England Pastoral," *Papers in Language and Literature* 7 (Fall 1971): 374–

81; Theodore Miller, "The Muddled Politics of Henry James's *The Bostonians*," *Georgia Review* 26 (1972): 336–46.

29. Judith Fetterly, "Henry James's Eternal Triangle," in *The Resisting Reader: A Feminist Approach to American Fiction* (Bloomington, IN: Indiana University Press, 1978), 132–34. Other sympathetic readings are given by Lillian Faderman, "Female Same-Sex Relationships in Novels by Longfellow, Holmes, and James," *New England Quarterly* 51 (1978): 309–32, and Nina Auerbach, *Communities of Women: An Idea in Fiction* (Cambridge, MA: Harvard University Press, 1978), 119–41.
30. Stone, 280; see also Long, "Society and the Masks."
31. Eakin, 337.
32. Eugene O'Neill, *Mourning Becomes Electra: A Trilogy* (New York: Horace Liveright, Inc., 1931); all page references to this edition.
33. See Virginia Ogden Birdsall, "Hawthorne's Fair-Haired Maidens: The Fading Light," *PMLA* 75 (June 1960): 250–56; and Gloria Chasson Erlich, "Deadly Innocence: Hawthorne's Dark Women," *New England Quarterly* 41 (June 1968): 163–79.
34. Nathaniel Hawthorne, *The Blithedale Romance and Fanshawe*, vol. 3 of The Centenary Edition of the Works of Nathaniel Hawthorne (Columbus, OH: Ohio State University Press, 1964); all page references to this edition.
35. Nina Baym, *"The Blithedale Romance*: A Radical Reading," *Journal of English and German Philology* 67 (1968): 562.
36. Birdsall, 254–55.
37. Nina Baym, *"The Blithedale Romance*: A Radical Reading," 561; see also Robert Stanton, "The Trial of Nature: An Analysis of *The Blithedale Romance*,"

PMLA 76 (December 1961): 528–38; Kent Bales, "The Allegory and the Radical Romantic Ethic of *The Blithedale Romance*," *American Literature* 46 (March 1974): 41–53, for readings that question the value of Priscilla's "spirituality."

38. Oliver Wendell Holmes, *Elsie Venner* (Boston: Houghton, Mifflin and Company, 1896); all page references to this edition.
39. Fryer, 29–40.
40. Fryer, 117. Professor Fryer originally makes this remark about Milly Theale.
41. Gail Godwin, *The Odd Woman* (New York: Berkley Publishing Co., 1976), 112.
42. John P. Marquand, *The Late George Apley*: *A Novel in the Form of a Memoir* (Boston: Little, Brown, & Co., 1938); all page references to this edition.
43. Edith Wharton, *Ethan Frome* (New York: Scribner's, 1911); all page references to this edition.
44. See Kenneth Bernard, "Imagery and Symbolism in *Ethan Frome*," *College English* 23 (December 1961): 178–84.

II

The Midwest

Chapter 3

Lisel Mueller and the Idea of Midwestern Poetry

By Paul Solyn

Any discussion of Midwestern poetry begins as a task of definition. In part this is because there is no school or movement that is accepted as Midwestern poetry, although there may be some benefit in that since the lack of a self-conscious school precludes arbitrary definitions. But the difficulty goes beyond the lack of a formal movement. If Midwestern poetry is defined as poetry written by Midwesterners, one must define the Midwest—no easy task in itself, for it is hard to argue that the industrial states of the Great Lakes have very much in common with the farming and ranching states of the Great Plains. For example, the population density of Indiana is eighty times that of South Dakota, and that is not the extreme case. It is especially significant that there is no longer a center of Midwestern letters, as Chicago may once have been; lacking such a center, there may be no consistency, no common ground, to writing in the Midwest.

Even if one defines the Midwest loosely as the states west of the thirteen colonies and east of the Rockies and not part of the South (itself a poorly defined region), one has difficulty categorizing Midwestern writers. William Wilson writes that it is hard enough to determine who is an Indiana author:

> *Or does one call Kenneth Rexroth and Samuel Yellen Hoosier poets, writers as unlike Riley and, at the same time, as unlike each other as any two poets could be, the one a native of South Bend but better known as the pundit of the best generation in San Francisco, the other a native of Lithuania but all his many pedagogic years a teacher at Indiana University? Ezra Pound once taught for a term at Wabash College; is he a Hoosier poet? (1)*

Multiply this by the number of states one supposes constitute the Midwest, and the problem seems insoluble.

Among Midwestern poets, Lisel Mueller stands virtually alone in her willingness to take on this task. She attempts to define Midwestern poetry in her essay, "Midwestern Poetry: Goodbye to All That," published in 1971 in the first volume of *Voyages to the Inland Sea,* an annual of Midwestern poetry published by the Murphy Library of the University of Wisconsin at La Crosse (2). Mueller's qualifications are appropriate for this: her critical articles have appeared repeatedly in *Poetry* and other magazines, and she has reviewed poetry for the Chicago *Daily News* since 1965. Her second collection of poems, *The Private Life*, was the Lamont Poetry Selection for 1975 and was published by the Louisiana State University Press in 1976.

Mueller's essay is, as the title suggests, essentially backward-looking, almost nostalgic. She begins by apologizing: "The idea of regional poetry seems an oddly old-fashioned one in this age," and then states that Midwestern poetry is "passing out of existence" (p. 1). It is for this reason that she wants to discuss what she sees as probably the last generation of identifiably Midwestern poets, those whose work is part of what she terms "a recognizable community of feeling." This community of feeling is passing out of existence, she writes, because of the homogenization of American life: "Our communal allegiances are short-lived, and why shouldn't they be, when one house, one street, one subdivision looks like any other?" It is not merely that regionalism is passé—although Mueller says that the idea of regional poetry seems old-fashioned, she does not argue that our time has any direct quarrel with regionalism—but rather that regional differences themselves are disappearing.

Although it is clear that American popular culture, particularly the national media culture, has contributed to a lessening of regional differences, it seems that this homogenization has not proceeded as fast as Mueller expected. For example, in the heyday of radio all its announcers were expected to speak as if they were from Ohio, but it is now common to hear in national television newscasts the accents of Texas and New York. Furthermore, the past two decades have seen poets throughout the country assume a posture of resistance to national culture; in this situation, regional differences may be cultivated not for themselves but because they are alternatives to the national culture. Mueller also writes, "I agree that customs and mores change surprisingly, sometimes frustratingly, little in this country. The question is how much poets—who are not, as you say, creatures of pop culture—will continue to reflect this" (Lisel Mueller, *personal communication,* September 5, 1975).

Mueller defines Midwestern poetry as owing its life and interests to the experience of a Midwest that very nearly suits the stereotypical (and perhaps Eastern) view of the Midwest:

> ... *the vast stretches of farmland, the rolling hills with their many shades of green, the great rivers and thousands of small lakes, the forests of Michigan, Minnesota, and Wisconsin, the towns with their rectangular layouts, their elm-shaded porches, their Elks Clubs, and their dreary Main Streets (p. 2).*

Essentially, this is the rural and small-town Midwest; the large cities, whatever their geographic location, are held to be atypical of this vague Midwestern ethos. "All large cities in this country are very similar; at least they share a great many more physical and cultural characeristics with each other than with their particular hinterlands" (p. 2).

On these grounds Mueller excludes all poets whose concerns and imagery are exclusively urban, although a footnote apologizes for the exclusion of several Chicago poets, chief among them Gwendolyn Brooks. But in the industrial states of the Midwest, the states bordering the Great Lakes, it is usual for 90 percent of the population to live on 10 percent of the land. Is it, after all, defensible to define Midwestern poetry in such a manner that the concerns of such a large part of the population will be excluded? Although Mueller does not take up this question directly, it follows from her argument that the poetry of the urban Midwest should not be markedly different from the poetry of any other urban area. From this one may infer that the poetry of the nonurban Midwest, which is what Mueller is talking about, does in some way differ. Further, it might be argued that the urban Midwest has been shaped by many of the same forces as the rural Midwest and shares the same attitudes.

The influences behind these attitudes include nineteenth-century settlement and the experience of the frontier; a predominantly Protestant population of British,

German, and Scandinavian ancestry; and, in particular, a society based on equality, individualism, and self-sufficiency. Lacking an entrenched aristocracy of religion, rank, culture, or wealth, settlers in the Midwest relied on practical reason and experience. Mueller writes, "It is unimaginable that, for example, transcendentalism or the art-for-art's-sake movement could have arisen in the Midwest (3). She adds that the overall political conseratism of the Midwest tolerated communal utopias along with other kinds of fierce and often radical independence, and notes that one of the overriding themes of Midwestern writing has been "the debasement of the pioneer heritage by industrial encroachment" (p. 3).

With such an emphasis on practical necessity, Midwestern writing has tended to be realistic rather than idealistic; optimism is not altogether foreign to it, but only Carl Sandburg could be optimistic about the growth of cities and the spread of industry. The Midwestern literary tradition does not, however, attempt to affirm the rural and small-town values that lie beneath most of it. "Masters' 'Spoon River,' on the other hand, was, like Anderson's 'Winesburg, Ohio,' faint with praise and heavy with denunciation of small-town life," Mueller writes (p. 4). Yet this disgust with small-town narrowness, as Barry Gross suggests, does not indicate a preference for the cities. Rather, it is a rejection of false sophistication and a denunciation of the rural Midwest's failure to live up to its own principles (4).

Despite its generally rural interests, Midwestern poetry does not tend to be pastoral. A comment by Thomas McGrath, a North Dakota poet who has also been associated with the San Francisco Renaissance (and who rejects regionalism on the ground that it is merely a variant of the national culture) is relevant here:

> *I'm not interested in nature in a nineteenth century sense—I don't have any pantheistic feelings about nature, I don't have any nature mysticism, I believe. I don't see nature as representing some kind of higher order of things. It's just for me something that's there, that is the ground of man's existence, and I think that without some sense of the goings-on of nature—things like seasonal changes, growth and death, and so on—a whole dimension of one's life is missing (5).*

Similarly, Mueller writes that Robert Bly's mystical sensibility, although rooted in his experience, is not especially typical of Midwestern poetry (p. 5). In the Midwest, nature is part of reality although not the whole of it, neither an escape from reality nor a set of symbols for it.

Mueller makes a few other important observations about Midwestern poetry. Its diction is generally plain, even without the relatively recent insistence on simple language—perhaps a result of the informal, egalitarian heritage. Mueller writes that "free verse, Midwest style, was not a European import, but rather an introduction of everyday common speech patterns into the province of poetry" (p. 7). This view is hardly unique to the Midwest, since it is more often said of William Carlos Williams and other poets of other regions. But Mueller's point is that in the Midwest this hardly seemed even noteworthy, since it is the direction in which the Midwestern tendency would run in any case. Furthermore, the "everyday common speech" of the Midwest is perhaps the plainest in the nation.

It could likewise be predicted that Midwestern poets would not be especially interested in poetic technique. This does not mean that Midwestern poets lack technical skill; rather, few seem to place much value on technical accomplishment for its own sake. In comparison with some of the poetry associated with other regions—the Fugitive poets of the South, for instance—Midwestern poetry may seem to lack technical proficiency. But its technique is adequate for its intentions. The difference is that a conspicuous show of technique is seldom an intention:

> *Verbal innovation has never made real headway here, and elegance of style has neither been a goal nor a fact. In the old battle between virtuosity and integrity of feeling—battle between paper tigers though it may be—allegiance has never been a problem: Midwestern poets believe that the exposed grain of experience is far more beautiful than any glossy finish (p. 7).*

Lacking most rhetorical flourishes, Midwestern poetry seems to depend more on the structure of the subject than on specifically poetic structures: fine as art may be, practical concerns take precedence.

The consuming interest in the relationship between people and their environment that precludes romanticization of nature leads to an interest in individuals; the character sketch, though hardly unique to the Midwest, has a special importance in Midwestern poetry. Mueller writes, "One keeps coming back, not to the 'human condition' in general, but to individual human lives" (p. 6), and adds, "This deeply ingrained humanism, this attention and respect accorded the individual person, may well be the special contribution of Midwestern poets to American poetry" (p. 7). The example and influence of Edgar Lee Masters cannot be underestimated, even though Edward Arlington Robinson had done much the same thing in New England. Masters is far more important as an influence, in part because he is a Midwesterner himself and because of the relative lack of an existing Midwestern tradition, but primarily because he is not only the beginning of a specifically literary tradition in the Midwest, but also the manifestation of a tradition that colored all of human life.

On the other hand, Mueller notes, Robinson—like Frost—stood outside much of his particular heritage. It is common for Midwestern poems, such as those of William Stafford, to deal not merely with people and landscape, but with people *in* the landscape: "Whether the environment is industrial or rural, man is what he is, in part at least, because of that environment" (p. 6). It might be added that people are part of that environment; what McGrath calls the "terrible isolation" of growing up in the Midwest may also have something to do with this.

The most serious weakness in Mueller's argument is not its limitation to a single generation of poets, the author's own, nor the deliberate exclusion of poets who, like Eliot and McClure and Koch, are strongly associated with other regions, but rather the exclusion of the urban Midwest, the large cities and the smaller industrial towns. Mueller argues that all large cities are very much alike, regardless of region. But it would seem likely that Indianapolis and Columbus, or Cincinnati and Milwaukee, are more like each other than any of these is like Boston or Atlanta. Nor is Chicago altogether like New York or Los Angeles, and it may be that these differences have to do with the same forces that would lead to other regional differences: although cities may differ greatly from their hinterlands, they also have much in common with them.

Mueller does cite one poem that deals with concerns that are as much urban as rural: James Wright's "Autumn Begins in Martins Ferry, Ohio," with its "gray faces of Negroes in the blast furnace at Benwood,/ And the night watchman of Wheeling Steel,/ Dreaming of heroes" (6). Wright's interests here are entirely consistent with Mueller's antiurban definition of Midwestern poetry. But it should be noted that Martins Ferry, although a small town (by 1970 its population had grown to 10,757) and the oldest white settlement in the state, is more a grimy industrial town than a farming village, as in fact Wright's imagery suggests. From this one may conclude that it might be possible to find in a purely urban poem the qualities that Mueller has described.

One poet whom Mueller does not mention whose work may be of interest in this connection is David Wagoner. His poem "A Valedictory to Standard Oil of Indiana," for instance, deals with the industrial blight, particularly that of the refineries, at East Chicago, and it is a valediction in the literal sense, a farewell wish, beginning with "In the darkness east of Chicago, the sky burns over the plumbers' nightmares/ Red and blue, and my hometown lies there loaded with gasoline." Yet the poem is concerned not so much with abstract environmentalism as with the personal relationships that are part of the situation:

> Standard Oil is canning my high school classmates
> And the ones who fell out of junior high or slipped in the grades.
> What should they do, gassed up in their Tempests and Comets, raring to go
> Somewhere with their wives scowling in front and kids stuffed in the back,
> Past drive-ins jammed like car-lots, trying to find the beaches
> But blocked by freights for hours, stopped dead in their tracks
> Where the rails, as thick as thieves along the lakefront,
> Lower their crossing gates to shut the frontier? What can they think about
> As they stare at the sides of boxcars for a sign (7)

and with the poet's own relationship to them: "As the Laureate of the Class of '44—which doesn't know it has one—/ I offer this poem" (8). It is because of this mild self-mockery and effacement, as well as the quiet, matter-of-fact tone of the lines that follow that the much-quoted last line of the poem, "Get out of town," has neither the rancor nor the fury that is sometimes ascribed to it, but is rather a simple and flat statement of the author's wish.

These poems suggest that Mueller's exclusion of poets whose concerns and imagery are predominantly urban is in fact an arbitrary one, and that her premises and conclusions about Midwestern poetry, its practical realism and humanism, may apply equally to Midwestern urban poetry. Important as this enlargement of scope may be, it is well that Mueller did not attempt it in her essay, since the case is probably more clearly stated without it. Nonetheless, the way in which Mueller's observations may be applied to cases she does not take up is a measure of the strength and accuracy of her argument.

A further weakness, more apparent now than when Mueller's essay was published in 1971, is her failure to discuss work by Midwestern women poets. Gwendolyn Brooks, the only woman cited, is included in the aforementioned footnote dealing with urban poets, but Mueller draws no examples from writing by women. The sources that Mueller claims for Midwestern poetry are, however, at least as available to women writers as to men, and the omission of poetry by women appears primarily to reflect a paucity of published work by Midwestern women that has only recently been remedied. Historically, of course, neither regional writing nor writing by women has enjoyed very wide distribution, and much important writing by Midwestern women has become available only within the past decade (9).

One such work is Ona Siporin's *Girl on a White Gate,* a performance poem for four voices published by Raintree Press in 1977:

> *you talk with the side of your tongue*
> *you say*
> > *i am confused   i have no power*
>
> *this is my chant*
> > *a woman begins as a girl*
> > *she runs through the fields in the fall*
> > *her arms at her sides like delicate wings*
> > *she knows summer*
> > *she knows snowstorms*
> > *she knows the smell of cottonwood in the spring*
> > *she knows the river at midnight*
>
> > *but the day a woman enjoys her first love*
> > *cuts her in two*
> > *from that time on she is another (10)*

Inevitably, one also looks to Mueller's own poems for examples. From her recent book *The Need to Hold Still*, published by Louisiana State University Press in 1980, comes "Another Version":

> *Our trees are aspens, but people*
> *mistake them for birches;*
> *they think of us as characters*
> *in a Russian novel, Kitty and Levin*
> *living contentedly in the country (11).*

The gentle mockery of literary self-dramatization is a quality that Mueller finds especially characteristic of Midwestern poetry. Later in the poem it turns to a serious end: "But like the three sisters, we rarely speak / of what keeps us awake at night." (12)

What, then, is the significance of Mueller's essay? First of all, it demonstrates that there is a Midwestern regional tradition in poetry. Second, it accomplishes what it attempts: to define and characterize a particular generation—loosely, the generation born between the wars—of Midwestern poets. Third, it has provided a rallying point for Midwestern writers who had all along felt some sort of regional affinity. A question about regionalism to many poets living in the Midwest will be answered with a reference to Mueller's essay. Finally, if Mueller's feeling that Midwestern poetry is dying should turn out to be wrong, it may, through encouragement of younger poets who feel Midwestern qualities in their writing, lead to a degree of continuity between the Midwestern poetry of the past and present and a Midwestern poetry of the future.

Mueller refers to many Midwestern poets in her essay, notably James Wright, Dave Etter, Thomas McGrath, and Theodore Roethke, and closes with a quotation from William Stafford. But Mueller's own poems speak equally clearly to this matter; the title of one, "A Real Toad in a Real Garden," might also be a summary of her essay. The end of her sequence of "Highway Poems," however, is most appropriate:

> *No, these are deathbed visits: regrets,*
> *surprising grief and sudden love,*
> *terror of loss, the need to lay*
> *hands on the past before it is gone;*
> *hold on to the knowledge at least, if not*
> *the stairs and walls of our history;*
> *walk away weeping at least, assured*
> *that sometime, a long time ago,*
> *we came from somewhere, that we are real (13).*

NOTES

1. William E. Wilson, *Indiana: A History* (Bloomington, IN.: Indiana University Press, 1966), 216.
2. Lisel Mueller, "Midwestern Poetry: Goodbye to All That," in *Voyages to the Inland Sea,* vol. 1, ed. John Judson (La Crosse, WI.: Center for Contemporary Poetry, Murphy Library, University of Wisconsin - La Crosse, 1971), 1–10. References to this essay are given in parentheses.
3. For a differing view see Douglas A. Noverr, "Midwestern Travel Literature of the Nineteenth Century," *Midamerica,* vol. IV, 1977, 23–25.
4. Barry Gross, "In Another Country: The Revolt from the Village," *Midamerica,* vol. IV, 1977, 108.
5. Mark Vinz, "Poetry and Place: An Interview with Thomas McGrath," in *Voyages to the Inland Sea,* vol. 3, ed. John Judson (La Crosse, WI.: Center for Contemporary Poetry, Murphy Library, University of Wisconsin - La Crosse, 1973), 34.
6. James Wright, *The Branch Will Not Break* (Middletown, CT.: Wesleyan University Press, 1963), 15.
7. David Wagoner, *Collected Poems* (Bloomington, IN.: Indiana University Press, 1976), 82.
8. Wagoner, 83.
9. Two of the best sources for Midwestern poetry are John Judson's Juniper Press and Fredric Brewer's Raintree Press (and its successor, The Private Press of Frederic Brewer). Juniper Press, in La Crosse, Wisconsin, publishes two series of chapbooks and a semiannual magazine, *Northeast,* and offers annual subscriptions to either or both; Judson was also the editor of *Voyages to the Inland Sea.* Raintree, located in Bloomington, Indiana, is newer and draws on a

smaller geographical area, but has published relatively more chapbooks by Midwestern women poets. Mueller also recommends the anthology *Heartland,* edited by Lucien Stryk (De Kalb, IL.: Northern Illinois University Press, 1967).

10. Ona Siporin, *Girl on a White Gate* (Bloomington, IN.: Raintree Press, 1977), 18.
11. Lisel Mueller, *The Need to Hold Still* (Baton Rouge, LA.: Louisiana State University Press, 1980), 5.
12. Mueller, *The Need to Hold Still,* 5.
13. Lisel Mueller, *The Private Life* (Baton Rouge, LA.: Louisiana State University Press, 1976), 10-11.

III

Appalachian Mountain Region

Chapter 4

Harriet Arnow's Kentucky Novels
Beyond Local Color

By Glenda Hobbs

Aside from specialists in American literature and women's studies, few people have heard of Harriette Arnow, and fewer still know any of her novels except *The Dollmaker* (1954). Writing about hill people from her native state of Kentucky, she is alternately labeled a "woman" or a "regional" writer. While it is generally conceded that the former tag is pejorative, few have considered the assumptions behind the term "regional." It is, I suspect, employed as condescendingly as the qualifier "woman": a "regionalist" can be "good" but only in a limited sphere.

A reason for the negative connotations of the classifier "regional" is its confusion with a more specialized term, "local color." While local color usually describes a nineteenth-century American literary movement, it can refer to any work whose author points out decorative regional details to add interest to the narrative. "Regional" works may include descriptions of landscape and customs, but they are intrinsic and crucial to an understanding of plot or character. Confusion arises when critics use the terms interchangeably or assume that any work containing a significant amount of regional detail must be merely highlighting the area's picturesqueness.

Perhaps, then, *The Dollmaker* is better known than Arnow's previous two novels because it is less obviously "regional," and has been spared the unfortunate blemish of the misused word. Three-fourths of the novel takes place in wartime Detroit, where the Nevels family migrates so the father can work in a factory and contribute to the "war effort." Arnow's first two novels, *Mountain Path* (1936) and *Hunter's Horn* (1949), are set entirely in rural Kentucky, and both describe hill people struggling with a barren, gully-ridden land, with a vestigial fundamentalist fatalism, and with their own tribalism. While enthusiastic critics lauded both novels, unknowingly they undermined their own praise and relegated the works to obscurity when they categorized them as "regional." Some, mistaking necessary descriptions for decoration, meant "local color"; others, assuming that any work rooted firmly in rural Kentucky must have only a limited appeal, used "regional" to mean folksy, and therefore of minor importance.

Mountain Path established Harriette Arnow as a writer whose gift was her poignant evocation of a poor but starkly beautiful "Appalachia" (1). The story of a city-bred college student who goes to a remote "hollow" to board with a hill family and teach in a one-room school, *Mountain Path* dramatizes the young woman's emotions as she learns to appreciate their familial devotion, their intimacy with the land, and their unique brand of justice.

Reviewers called the book a "good regional novel." One tried to account for its appeal: "There is something in the beauty and isolation of the setting, in its traditional lawlessness, in the archaic speech and customs of its people, which makes it an excellent background for romance—for romance of passion and violence on the one hand, or of poetic imagination on the other" (2). Authors can do without "praise" that applauds the quaintness, the picturesqueness of a land and its delightfully rustic people. Arnow's exact dialect is hardly "archaic," and the "tradition" of feuding is portrayed as horrifying and unromantic.

Even such an astute critic as Alfred Kazin, who noted the novel's "spiritual indignation" and "power," thought it a marvelous novel "of its type" (3). While most southern regional novels, he felt, concentrate more on background than on people and document an area without any larger design, he applauded *Mountain Path's* concern with the way setting affects people's lives. But Kazin still objected to one of the novel's most "regional" aspects; he wondered why "every novel written about Kentucky must have a feud in it" (4). Arnow's inclusion of the feud is not gratuitous or merely colorful. It is used to demonstrate the heroine's transformation: initially outraged by the thought of justifiable killing, she is shocked to find herself demanding vengeance on her hosts' enemies. The other reason for its inclusion seems obvious: even in the 1930s feuds were a fact of life in remote corners of southeastern Kentucky.

When critics saw that Arnow's second novel focused on a Kentucky hill man obsessed with fox hunting, they were quick to hail *Hunter's Horn* for its realistic depiction of a quaint old mountain custom. This novel, too, was called an "unusually good book of its kind. This is partly because the details of life in rural Kentucky are described with authority" (5). One wonders how Melville would have felt if *Moby Dick* were praised only for its accurate documentation of whale-hunting, for Arnow's book is as little "about" fox hunting as Melville's is about whaling. Nunn Ballew searches for the elusive red fox, King Devil, with as maniacal a compulsion as Ahab stalks Moby Dick. Arnow's talent makes Little Smokey Creek as vast a territory as the

Pacific Ocean. A handful of critics perceived *Hunter's Horn*'s "fine, strong, frame of universality" (6), but most damned it with tainted praise. One critic said it was his "candidate for the Pulitzer Prize"; it was, he argued, "a really remarkable regional novel" (7).

The Dollmaker escaped the label. It was called "an important new novel" (8) and "an unflinching and compassionate novel of contemporary America" (9). (Contemporary America must exclude nonindustrial areas, for Arnow had always written about contemporary Kentucky.) *The Dollmaker* was unanimously hailed as a masterwork. Harnett T. Kane's remarks in the *New York Times Book Review* are representative of its critical reception: "If 1954 produces more than one or two novels of this power and compassion, it's a banner year" (10).

It is ironic that critics did not call this novel "regional," because more than Arnow's other novels, *The Dollmaker* probes the way of life and the character of Kentucky hill people. She dramatizes the difficulty of safeguarding one's religion, of deriving strength from nature, and of preserving pride in one's dialect and native crafts in an alien culture. Perhaps a novel is considered regional only if all the action occurs in the same rural setting. By allowing her hill people to leave Kentucky and go to a northern city, Arnow silenced critics who intimated parochialism by calling her early novels regional.

But the label has stuck. Because Harriette Arnow and other modern "regionalists" are seen as literary descendants of the local colorists, they are considered technicians of a minor mode. Critics believe them to continue their predecessors' preoccupation with the quaint, the picturesque, and the sentimental. Although the precise dates for the local color movement vary (roughly from 1865 to 1900), its literary reputation does not. After the Civil War, increased mobility fostered an upsurge of curiosity about life in all parts of the country. At the same time, growing industrialism caused people to look closely at a rapidly fading agrarian culture; they began to feel nostalgia for the individuality of isolated sections that would soon become standardized.

As a result, local color literature became touristic. Often written by outsiders, it self-consciously pointed out the uniqueness of various rural pockets, usually exaggerating idiosyncrasies to make the section seem more "quaint." Dialect, dress, customs, and landscape were conscientiously and excessively documented, and the author's attitude was often patronizing. Characters could be ridiculed or affectionately mocked, as long as they were "colorful." Those writers who escaped much of the condescending naturalism of local color—Kate Chopin, Mary E. Wilkins Freeman, Sarah Orne Jewett—were either called masters of that mode or were said to transcend it entirely. Modern regionalists should not be judged for their mistaken connection to the local colorists. Not all precursors are ancestors; anyone who must name literary sires should consider Mark Twain rather than Bret Harte.

While critics of regional literature assert that an author preoccupied with Kentucky (or any other rural area) ignores Athens and Rome, its advocates argue that Athens and Rome can only be reached through Kentucky, Nebraska, or Yoknapatawpha. As one partisan puts it, regionalism is not "an ultimate in literature, but . . . a first step . . . the coming to close knowledge about the life of a region in which [the writer] lives as a first necessity for sound writing, even as knowledge of oneself—'know thyself'—is also a first necessity. The 'universal' when healthy, alive, pregnant with values, springs inevitably from the specific fact" (11).

Some supporters of regional literature believe that "universal" works must evoke a recognizable locale. One such group was the self-styled Agrarians, who advocated the economic and social superiority of ruralism over industrialism and applauded Southern writers who celebrated rural life. "Regionalism," wrote Donald Davidson, "is not an end in itself, not a literary affectation, not an aesthetic credo, but a condition of literary realization. The function of a region is to endow the American artist with character and purpose" (12). Davidson and his fellow Agrarians felt that any work unrooted in a particular time and place loses its humanity and evaporates into abstraction. While they argued persuasively for the strengths of regional literature, they failed to acknowledge the possibility that a work with a nebulous setting could dramatize recognizable emotions and dilemmas. They would deny the power of Beckett's *Waiting for Godot* and Kafka's *The Trial* on theoretical grounds.

An ideological commitment to regionalism could cause a writer to sacrifice idea and character to descriptive detail. It is the use, rather than the accumulation of regional material, Robert Penn Warren wrote, that determines literary merit (13). The life of a region should be the medium of expression, not the message. Hence, "The theoretically perfect regionalist must be someone like Mary Austin, but the best regional literature is something like 'The Adventures of Huckleberry Finn,' which is not theoretically regional at all" (14).

Ideally, a writer intimately connected to the history and culture of a particular community sees peculiarities of a region as givens, as points of departure, not as oddities to be explained or "expressed." Such writers perceive their neighbors from an insider's perspective. Mary Austin, whose essays provide better arguments for regional writing than her fiction, explains that a writer's "regional environment . . . forces upon him behavior patterns such as earliest become the habit of blood, the unconscious factor of adjustment in all his mechanisms. Of all the responses of his psyche none pass so soon and surely as these into that field of consciousness from which all invention and creative effort of every sort proceed" (15).

Arnow does not write about Kentucky any more than Twain wrote about Missouri. These writers create art from experiences that include details of memory and observation, but their backgrounds are more important for the ideas and attitudes that have evolved over generations. A writer cannot deny her heritage. Living in a close-knit community gives the writer a special focus—what Arnow calls "a sense of belonging" (16)—and creates a world of moral choice the characters accept or protest against. Arnow's fiction demonstrates her belief that character is more important than setting: "I had to have some setting because the people were either at one with the setting or rebelling against it" (17).

In Allen Tate's famous essay "Regionalism and Sectionalism" (1931), he describes the distinction between conscious sectionalism and an awareness of tradition:

> *By regionalism, then, I mean only the immediate organic sense of life in which a fine artist works . . . tradition has nothing to do with "expressing" a region, though of course tradition is always local in origin. The most traditional of writers can use all of his personal tradition, it is indeed inescapable that he should use it, without ever writing abut the society, the region, the nation, from which his tradition is derived. To write traditionally is not to use local color or one's past; it is the assumption that people up to a certain point will behave in a manner to which one is accustomed. . . . From this point of view a great deal of regional literature is the very contradiction of traditional writing. A self-conscious regionalism destroys tradition with its*

> *perpetual discovery of it; makes it clumsy and sterile. And regionalism in this sense, when it merges with sectionalism, is death to literature. Sectionalism is politics (18).*

Arnow's work is "traditional" by Tate's definition. She is not interested in pointing out the uniqueness of her region; she is a native Kentuckian who understands how the Kentucky hills and hollows affect the attitudes and the psychology of her characters.

Both advocates and critics of regionalism are mistaken when they assign values to a term that must be purely descriptive if it is to inform rather than to confuse. Reviewers of Arnow's early novels who called them good novels "of that type" implied her provinciality. But supporters who hailed her novels *because* they were "regional" did her as great a disservice: they suggested that only those readers with sectional pride could fully appreciate her work.

Harriette Arnow's first three novels should no more be read because they are "regional" than because she is a "woman writer." Her contribution to literature is her harshly moving portrayal of people struggling to maintain their integrity in an oppressive, often hostile environment, wherever they find it. But citizens of any world will find her novels more gripping because her characters' dilemmas grow out of the "habits of blood" they acquired from generations in the Kentucky hills. Attempts to break those habits—Reuben's carrying a knife, or Cassie's talking with her imaginary playmate Callie Lou—are met with deep and often fatal resistance. Perhaps Arnow will begin to receive her due acclaim when critics realize that she has gone far beyond local color. Labels like "regional" do not trouble Arnow's readers, who find it difficult to recover their own worlds once they have entered hers.

NOTES

1. Natives of the southern Appalachian Mountain region object to the term "Appalachia." Used by sociologists studying the hill poor, it is, they feel, condescending and does not take into account any differences among the seven states the term encompasses.
2. Margaret Wallace, "'Mountain Path' and Some Other Recent Works of Fiction," *New York Times Book Review,* 30 Aug. 1936, 6.
3. Alfred Kazin, "Diverse Themes in Fall Fiction," *New York Herald Tribune Books,* 6 Sept. 1936, 10–11.
4. Kazin, 11.
5. John Farrelly, "Fiction Parade," *New Republic*, 1 Aug. 1949, 26.
6. Florence Haxton Bullock, "Kentucky Hill Folk, Vividly Seen," *New York Herald Tribune Books,* 25 June 1949, 5.
7. Robert W. Henderson, *Library Journal* 74 (1 May 1949): 735.
8. Earle F. Walbridge, *Library Journal* 79 (15 March 1954): 550.
9. Walter Havighurst, "Hillbilly D.P.'s" *Saturday Review,* 24 April 1954, 12.
10. Harnett T. Kane, "The Transplanted Folk," *New York Times Book Review,* 25 April 1954, 4.
11. "Expression in Northwest Life," *New Mexico Quarterly* (May 1934): 128–29.
12. Donald Davidson, "Regionalism and Nationalism in American Literature," *American Review* 5 (April 1935): 61.
13. Warren warns of the hazards of willful regionalism in two articles: "Not Local Color," *Virginia Quarterly Review* 8:1 (1932): 153–60; and "Some Don'ts for

Literary Regionalists," *American Review* 8 (1936): 142–150.
14. "Regionalism or the Coterie Manifesto," *Saturday Review of Literature* 28 Nov. 1936, 8.
15. Mary Austin, "Regionalism in American Fiction," *English Journal* 21 (Feb. 1932): 97–106.
16. Harriette S. Arnow, "Some Musings on the Nature of History," *Historical Society of Michigan Publication: The Clarence M. Burton Memorial Lecture* (1968): 6.
17. Diana Orban, "Harriette Arnow Reflects on a Writer's Life," *Ann Arbor News*, 2 Nov. 1969, 13–24.
18. Allen Tate, "Regionalism and Sectionalism," *New Republic*, 23 December 1931, pp. 158–161.

Chapter 5

Widening Perspectives, Narrowing Possibilities
The Trapped Woman in Edith Summers Kelley's WEEDS

By Charlotte Goodman

Posterity has been kinder to Edith Summers Kelley, author of *Weeds* and the posthumous *The Devil's Hand,* than to many other authors whose novels are moderately praised by reviewers and then forgotten. Her novel, *Weeds,* originally published in 1923 by Harcourt Brace, was reissued in hard cover in 1972 for the Lost American Fiction series of Southern Illinois University Press, with Matthew Bruccoli as editor; in paperback in 1975 by Popular Library; and in 1982 by the Feminist Press; and *The Devil's Hand* was published by Southern Illinois in 1974.

Until that time, if Edith Summers Kelley's name was known at all, it was probably from the 12 entries about her that appear in Mark Schorer's biography of Sinclair Lewis. Kelley met Sinclair Lewis when she was secretary to Upton Sinclair at Helicon Hall, the short-lived experimental community that Sinclair founded; she was briefly engaged to Lewis (1), and then married his friend, Allan Updegraff. She continued to correspond with Lewis throughout her life, and it was Lewis who initially persuaded Harcourt Brace to publish *Weeds*, even offering his services as editor. Many years later Lewis was still championing *Weeds*, for he tried to persuade The Reader's Club, of which he was a member, to reissue it (2). Lewis would no doubt have been delighted to learn of Matthew Bruccoli's success not only in reviving *Weeds* but in having a second novel by Kelley published as well.

Yet such are the vagaries of literary success that merely republishing an author's work will not necessarily guarantee her a permanent place among those writers whose works continue to be read (3). Favorable reviews too are no guarantors of a lasting reading public: witness the fact that Joseph Wood Krutch's favorable review of *Weeds* in *The Nation* in 1924 failed to secure a second printing for the novel (4). What is needed is the kind of critical attention that will place the writer within a tradition, illuminate a writer's methods, and ultimately demonstrate her worth to those scholars and teachers who are responsible for drawing up syllabi and introducing literary works to new generations of readers. My motive for writing this article, therefore, is to give Edith Summers Kelley the critical attention I think she deserves; otherwise, I fear she may all too quickly become "lost" again, despite the earnest attempts of Sinclair Lewis initially and Matthew Bruccoli more recently to gain her a wider audience.

Kelley's attitude toward fiction is discernible in a passage in *Weeds* in which one of her characters speaks disparagingly of "purveyors of roseate fiction" whose romances, invariably about rich people, always end when their heroines get married (5); and in *The Devil's Hand*, when her protagonist, Rhoda Malone, says about popular Western novels, "They all seem so silly; the people in them and the things that happen are not a bit like real life" (6). In contrast to the writers of popular romance, whose sentimental love stories about people in high life "abounded in beautiful heroines with delicate hands that had never approached a dish rag or a hoe handle" (7), Kelley saw her task as that of writing realistic fiction about ordinary working class people.

Kelley knew the life she describes in her novels from first-hand experience, for after her marriage to Updegraff dissolved, she became the common-law wife of Fred Kelley, an artist and farmer, and they were tenant tobacco farmers like the Blackfords in *Weeds*; then they raised chickens in California where *The Devil's Hand* takes place. Her novels give us an accurate and detailed picture of the sights and sounds of farm life. She faithfully reproduces the dialect of her rural characters, and she depicts the workaday routine, the cycle of the seasons, the occasional feast or trip to town or visit with a neighbor that relieved the everyday monotony. She emphasizes as well the precariousness of earning one's living from the soil. The authenticity of her portraits of the tenant farmers in *Weeds* and the heterogeneous Californians in *The Devil's Hand* contributes to the effectiveness of her writing.

The central issue in both of Kelley's novels is the fate of the sensitive woman whose spirit rebels against the strictures imposed by biological, social, and economic factors. It is not surprising that Kelley, whose experience at Helicon Hall included participation in frequent discussions about women's rights (8), should have been particularly interested in the handicaps imposed on women. The young women who are the protagonists of her novels seek wider horizons than life ordinarily allows to females of their class and culture. In their struggles to preserve their identity and to achieve some measure of independence, they share a common experience with the rural women depicted in the novels of three of Kelley's contemporaries: *Country People* by Ruth Suckow; *Barren Ground* by Ellen Glasgow; and *The Time of Man* by Elizabeth Maddox Roberts (9).

In this article I will focus on *Weeds*, which is certainly Kelley's masterpiece. From the first chapter of *Weeds* it is evident that Judith Pippinger, Kelley's protagonist, is distinguishable from the other girls in her Kentucky farm community by her greater energy and assertiveness. "Land, that little gal's got life enough for a dozen sech—too much life, too much life for a gal!" observes Mr. Pippinger about his daughter as he sees her driving the mules out of the cornfield "with much whooping, armwaving, and bad language" (page 14). Judith, a dark-haired, mischievous tomboy, resembles Maggie Tulliver in George Eliot's *The Mill on the Floss*; like Maggie, she scandalizes her female relatives because of her "contempt for the decent and domestic" (page 25). Preferring her father's occupations and company to those of her mother and her two docile sisters, she chooses to spend her time in the fields rather than the kitchen.

As the novel progresses, it becomes increasingly obvious that the very qualities of energy and assertiveness that distinguish Judith from her counterparts are the qualities that will prevent her from accommodating herself to the only role her society allows for its women: that of a wife and mother. The child Judith, who shows "signs of an energy that craved constant outlet" (page 15), and the adolescent Judith, who defends her right to run about and swear like the boys, becomes the mature woman who rebels against her enslavement to the needs of her growing brood of children and the tedium that is her lot as the wife of a poor tobacco farmer.

In the world that Kelley describes, the chief anodyne for the monotony of everyday existence is sex. Young girls pore over the mail order' catalogs and picture themselves attracting admiring male glances when they are dressed in the splendid clothes they see there; women vicariously share the adventures of heroines in books with titles like *No Wedding Bells for Her,* and eagerly read articles like "How to Charm Those Whom You Meet and Love"; and the life of man is said to turn "flame colored when he ... learns to know the love o' wimmin" (page 309). Mating and procreation seem to be the chief business of the human world as well as the barnyard. Thus, the underlying function of a Christmas Eve party, which Kelley documents in great detail, is shown to be the promotion of romances among the young people, in order to ensure the continuity of the community. The elaborate preliminary preparations of Judith and her sisters include the purchase of material for new dresses, dresses that make them feel "somehow like different beings, as though they were not workaday people at all but ladies who had always worn new, fluffy dresses, white stockings, and shiny shoes" (page 83). On the evening of the party, the squalid, everyday surroundings, like the young women, seem transformed: the poor farmhouse where the party is held looks to the young women like a "house of many little golden windows" (page 85). It is obvious that the party has fulfilled its biological function when, immediately afterward, Judith's sister announces her engagement and Jerry Blackford begins to court Judith.

At the same time that Kelley is describing the merrymaking of the young folks, she introduces a note of pessimism that will be borne out by the subsequent chapters of the novel. Side by side with the "dancing girls in their slippers and light dresses" (page 87) and the guffawing, healthy young men are the "old folks"—those under fifty and mostly in their thirties and forties—who are said by Kelley to present "a scarecrow array of bent limbs, bowed shoulders, sunken chests, twisted contortions, and jagged angularities" (page 91). Even in the faces of the young girls, she observes, is "an old, patient, settled look, as though a black dress and a few gray hairs would make them sisters instead of daughters of the older women" (page 85). Busy with dancing and coquetting, the perceptive Judith fails to take note of those women whom the omniscient author points out to the reader:

> . . . *the skinny, dried-up little women in their black dresses and white aprons did not get much enjoyment out of the dance. There was neither allure nor mystery about the other sex for them any more; and they were disgusted and nauseated by the foul whiskey breath that spewed out upon them from their partners' mouths. The thought of the hard-earned money thrown away upon said whiskey did not tend to make them any more cheerful. They went through the dance as they had gone through everything else since childhood, as a matter of course, because the circumstances of their life demanded it (pages 91– 92).*

The mothers here foreshadow what their daughters will become.

Although Kelley describes how difficult life is for the men in the rural Kentucky community depicted in *Weeds*, the main direction of the novel is toward showing the toll that such an existence exacts from its women. "But seems like folks hain't in this world to git what they want, 'specially wimmin," says a horsetrader's wife (page 179). The novel begins with a description of a Sunday family gathering during which the men congregate in the barnyard to discuss the weather, the crops, and the neighbors; the children play hide-and-seek; while the women cook and wash dishes in the house. The fourth chapter of the novel describes the death of Judith's mother from pneumonia, which she contracted after doing a big washing in hot suds and getting chilled hanging out the clothes in the bitter winter wind.

Subsequently, Kelly shows the adverse effects of biological stresses and household responsibilities on Judith once she settles into the role of wife to Jerry Blackford. In contrast to the stereotypical image of the satisfied earth-mother type of character that is so often found in the fiction of the period (10), Kelley's protagonist is depressed after her baby's birth (11), feeling herself in "bondage" to "his insistent demands night and day for her continual presence at his side and for all sorts of constantly recurring small attentions" (page 159).

While the year and a half after the birth of the baby leaves no noticeable changes in Jerry, Kelley says that it destroys in Judith "the buoyancy and effervescence of youth" (page 159). Unlike her sister, who beams with maternal pride at her own spotless house and neat children, Judith loathes housework and feels stifled by the never-ending demands of her growing family. The oppressive burdens of housewives like her, who live in isolated shanties and never ever have a holiday, are movingly enumerated by Kelley in a passage whose cadenced prose almost has the ring of a ballad. Some of the chores listed by Kelley include the following:

> *Families must be fed after some fashion or other and dishes washed three times a day, three hundred and sixty-five days a year. Babies must be fed and washed and dressed and "changed" and rocked when they cried and kept out of mischief and danger. . . . Fires must be lighted and kept going as long as needed for cooking, no matter how great the heat. Cows must be milked and cream skimmed and butter churned. Hens must be fed and eggs gathered and the filth shoveled out of*

> henhouses. Diapers must be washed . . . floors must be swept. *(page 195)*

One of the ways in which Kelley emphasizes that for women like Judith, who practice no methods of birth control, biology does, in fact, equal destiny is through her description of Judith's physical and psychological reaction to each pregnancy. With her very first pregnancy the animated Judith is transformed into a languid creature who is sickened by kitchen smells and even the sight and odor of the gaudy nasturtiums in her garden. Her physical symptoms appear to symbolize her rejection of the maternal role. When she complains to a neighbor that "a caow ain't sick when she's a-fixin' to have a calf" (page 147), Judith draws a distinction between her own reactions to pregnancy and those of the barnyard creatures whom she has observed all of her life. During a subsequent pregnancy she exults in her "unnatural" loathing of the idea of having to bring up another baby, thinking: "The women who liked caring for babies could call her unnatural if they liked. She wanted to be unnatural. She was glad she was unnatural. Their nature was not her nature and she was glad of it" (page 240).

Ironically, her one attempt to add some excitement to her life, a summer romance with an itinerant evangelist, results in yet another unwanted pregnancy, which she manages to abort only by wading into an icy pool of water. Finally Judith decides to become "mistress of her own body" by abstaining from sexual relations altogether. Kelley comments, "She wanted no more children that she could not clothe, that she could hardly feed, that were a long torture to bear and a daily fret and anxiety after they were born" (page 299).

In addition to dramatizing in her novel the difficulties that accrue to women because of their biological role, Kelley also points out the ways in which a patriarchal culture has imposed unfair social restrictions on its women. This novel, written in 1923, in fact, raises some of the same issues that appear in the writings of today's feminists. Through her protagonist, whose point of view dominates much of the novel, Kelley articulates an awareness that women often are the losers in a society where roles are rigidly sex-determined. The young Judith, whose father describes her as "more a boy'n a gal" (page 34), complains when he condones the use of vulgar language from his son but criticizes her for swearing (12). She is also angered when her brother is permitted to sit rocking by the stove, "safe and aloof in his masculinity," while his sisters do the dishes, a chore from which he as a boy is excused (page 27).

The issue of housework is raised again later in the novel when Judith, after being confined to bed with influenza, discovers that her husband has completely neglected the household chores during her illness, allowing dirty dishes and unwashed clothes to accumulate. In response to her angry remonstrance he says, "Well, I don't claim to be no expert pot wrastler ner wet nurse neither," and he angrily tells her, "Aw, shet up. You're too damn fussy" (page 223). It is clear in this scene that Judith is the one who has the sympathies of the author.

The inequities of the patriarchal social system are symbolized in a scene in which Kelley describes the respective reactions of Judith and her husband Jerry to hog-killing day. Happily warming his hands above the fire, Jerry says to his friend Joe, "There hain't no day I like better'n hog-killing day!" (page 236). He explains that not only does he enjoy dressing the hog, but he also looks forward to a day of companionship with his friend who has come to help him. Judith, on the other hand, is revolted by her part of the job. Nauseated because she is pregnant and on edge because of the antics of her mischievous three-year-old, she gags and reels as she looks into the tub full of steaming guts. Kelley's words convey powerfully Judith's sense of revulsion:

> *The bluish viscera, bubbling up in innumerable little rounded blobs, filled it almost to overflowing. Bloody fragments emerged along with masses of intestines. The outside of the tub was daubed and streaked with blood. An unspeakable stench rose from it. (page 238)*

Unable to face the odious chore of rendering the guts in the tub, Judith announces, "It can stay there till it rots afore I'll tech a hand to it" (page 239). Kelley notes Jerry's reaction of bewilderment because Judith has challenged his authority, and his embarrassment "at this open affront from his wife before another man" (page 239). Fleeing from the house, Judith muses indignantly that the men were trying to foist upon her the only part of the job that was "tedious and hateful" (page 240).

Another facet of the social system that Kelley touches upon is the issue of economic inequities. Early in the novel when Judith quits her job as a hired hand on a neighbor's farm, the farmer's wife observes that now she will have to pay a male hired hand four times as much as Judith was earning (page 82). Another neighbor, Hat Wolf, expresses anger at the injustice of her own economic situation. "The men sholy do have it easy compared to us wimmin, Judy," she says.

> *Here all this summer I worked like a dawg in the terbaccer a settin' an' a toppin' an a hoein' an' a-wormin' an' a-cuttin'; an' all the fore part o' the winter I'll spend a-strippin'. An' then along about Christmas Luke'll haul the terbaccer off to Lexington an' sell it an' put the*

money in his pocket an' I won't see a dollar of it. (page 145)

Hat goes on to complain that her husband not only controls the money in the family but also decides what is and what is not "wimmin's work." To Hat he assigns the unpleasant task of picking geese feathers and then pockets the money when the feathers are sold. Furthermore, though she works as hard on the farm as he does, she also has the additional burdens of cooking and washing dishes and cleaning the house and doing the washing and tending the fowl.

The prevailing images in this novel about the defeat of a free spirit are those that contrast open and closed spaces, and vitality with stasis or death. Kelley describes Judith's love of being out of doors and, conversely, her dislike of the insides of houses, which stifle and depress her. Confined in the house with her new baby during the long winter months when the sun rarely shines, Judith draws pictures of "the sweep of hilltop lining itself against the sky" (page 161). Her feelings of being trapped in the dark, crowded tenant house, which looks to her "like a weathered packing case into which someone had sawed two or three holes" (page 243), find release only when she flees to the open country. Her eyes "instinctively reaching out for freedom" seek "the long view that sweeps from the top of the ridge to the horizon" (page 240).

Judith's fate is prefigured early in the novel as Kelley describes the sad fate of the minnows, butterflies, mud turtles, and grasshoppers that the young child tries to domesticate in an assortment of containers; the "curse of blight and disaster" (page 18) that befalls them will befall her too when she becomes a prisoner of her tenant shanty as an adult. Like the tender plants that are choked by the weeds from which the book gets its title, Judith, called a "poppy among weeds" (page 88), is gradually overwhelmed by the inexorable pressures of life. The determinism that pervades the novel is reflected in Judith's comment about her daughter, a comment that would apply to herself as well: "In every way she was a product of the life that had brought her into being, and that life would claim her to the end" (page 321).

Although Kelley's novel does not end with the suicide of her protagonist, as do so many novels about rebellious women, its ending is bleak nevertheless. With the death of Uncle Jabez, Judith loses the one person with whom she is able to communicate. Uncle Jabez, an elderly, philosophizing fiddler, and Judith, the farm girl who enjoys sketching people and animals and scenery in her spare moments, possess the sensibility of the artist (13). The young woman and the old man share a common pessimistic vision of the human condition: Uncle Jabez expresses the belief that the lucky ones are the ones who die young, for "they don't live long enough to find out haow little there is to make life worth livin'" (page 231); and Judith, observing a fly her dust rag has mashed and mangled, thinks bitterly, "What are we all anyway but flies?" (page 297). At the end of the novel Kelley portrays Judith as sadly reconciled to the inevitability of her fate and convinced of the uselessness of rebellion. Although she decides to return to her estranged husband's bed, she still feels herself to be like "a dog tied to a strong chain" (page 330), and sees a future of unrelieved monotony stretching out before her.

Like the realistic/naturalistic novels of John Steinbeck and Theodore Dreiser, *Weeds* focuses on the lives and hardships of working-class people. Kelley's contribution to the twentieth-century American novel is her compassionate presentation of the stresses of farm life from the point of view of a sensitive female protagonist. Not only does Edith Summers Kelley succeed in *Weeds* in dramatizing the biological and emotional struggles of her protagonist, Judith Pippinger, but she also points out some of the inequities of a patriarchal culture that prevents its women from realizing their full human potential.

NOTES

1. Schorer quotes Kelley as saying that she was the model for Leora Tozer in Lewis's *Arrowsmith*. See Mark Schorer, *Sinclair Lewis: An American Life* (New York: McGraw Hill, 1961), 420.
2. Schorer, 679.
3. Elaine Showalter wrote in "Review Essay: Literary Criticism," *Signs* (Winter 1975): 444: "Without critical attention Kelley and other women writers may quickly become lost to us."
4. *The Nation* 118 (1924): 65.
5. Edith Summers Kelley, *Weeds* (Illinois: Southern Illinois University Press, 1972), 120; all page references to this edition.
6. Edith Summers Kelley, *The Devil's Hand* (Illinois: Southern Illinois University Press, 1974), 53.
7. *Weeds,* 131.
8. Schorer, 113.
9. For a discussion of the relationship between *Weeds* and other novels about rural American women, see Charlotte Goodman, "Images of American Rural Women in the Novel," *University of Michigan Papers in Women's Studies* 1 (June 1975): 54–71.
10. Compare, for example, Kelley's vision of Judith's life with Willa Cather's more romantic view of Antonia surrounded by her lovely family at the end of *My Antonia.*
11. For an account of the way her publisher, Harcourt

Brace, insisted that she delete a scene describing the birth of Judith's first child, see Charlotte Goodman, "Afterword," *Weeds* (New York: The Feminist Press, 1982), 361. This scene is included in an appendix to the Feminist Press edition, 335–351.

12. Kelley's publishers insisted that she delete the "poor little handful of bad words" she had included deliberately to render a truer picture of the tobacco growers' language. (Letter to Alfred Harcourt, April 21, 1923, courtesy of Patrick Kelley.)

13. For a discussion of Judith Pippinger as an "artiste manqueé," see Charlotte Goodman, "Portraits of the Artiste Manqueé by Three Women Novelists," *Frontiers: A Journal of Women's Studies* 5 (Fall 1980), pp. 57–59.

IV

The South

Chapter 6

Alice Dunbar-Nelson
New Orleans Writer

By Roger Whitlow

Alice Dunbar-Nelson's contributions to American literature are unique, and she herself is distinctive for four major reasons: (1) she was a frequently published Black writer at the turn of the century; (2) she was married to the most gifted Black writer of his age, Paul Laurence Dunbar; and was, as Eugene Metcalf accurately says, "eclipsed by her husband's fame" (1); (3) she was an early and vocal advocate of women's rights; and (4) most significant for this study, she was, like Kate Chopin and George Washington Cable, an explorer of and writer about the New Orleans area and the peoples found there.

Alice Ruth Moore was only 20 when she published her first collection of short stories, *Violets and Other Tales,* in 1895. In the year after her marriage to Paul Laurence Dunbar she published another collection, *The Goodness of St. Rocque and Other Stories* (1899), under the name Alice Dunbar. She became Alice Dunbar-Nelson after Dunbar's death in 1906 and her subsequent marriage to Robert J. Nelson in 1916, and her later works include books "on race," such as *Masterpieces of Negro Eloquence* (1914) and *People of Color in Louisiana* (1916–17), and poetic and prose contributions to such magazines as *Lippincott's, Crisis, McClure's, Age, Women's Era, Monthly Review,* and *Colored American.* Alice Dunbar-Nelson was, in short, a prolific regional writer who has been almost completely overlooked.

Mrs. Dunbar-Nelson's ties to New Orleans were strong. She was born there in 1875, attended public school there throughout the 1880s, received a two-year teacher's degree from Straight College and later taught elementary school in the city, and, finally, used New Orleans as the setting for nearly all the short stories in her first two books. Metcalf says that by 1895 "she had already attracted a considerable local following in the New Orleans area, and her writing was known to the readers of a number of journals" (2). And later he says: "It was as both a social activist and writer that Alice made her reputation. A social figure no less important than her friends Mary Church Terrell and Victoria Earle Matthews, she was also, like another of her acquaintances, Charlotte Forten Grimké, a competent literary artist" (3).

Mrs. Dunbar-Nelson's New Orleans stories fall generally into four categories: those treating unsuccessful love, those dealing with quietly tragic heroism, those dealing with women's rights, and those outlining ethnic portraits. Two of the most typical unrequited-love stories are "Violets" and "A Story of Vengeance," both from her 1895 volume, *Violets and Other Tales,* the purpose of which she modestly explains at the opening: "If perchance this collection of idle thoughts may serve to while away an hour or two, or lift for a brief space the load of care from someone's mind, their purpose has been served—the author is satisfied" (4).

The title story, "Violets," opens with a nameless young

lady preparing to send a bouquet of violets to her lover, with the following letter:

> *Dear, I send you this little bunch of flowers as my Easter token. Perhaps you may not be able to read their meaning, so I'll tell you. Violets, you know, are my favorite flowers. Dear, little human-faced things! They seem always as if about to whisper a love-word; and then they signify that thought which passes always between you and me. . . . The violets and pinks are from a bunch I wore to-day, and when kneeling at the altar, during communion, did I sin, dear, when I thought of you? The tube-roses and orange-blossoms I wore Friday night; you always wished for a lock of my hair, so I'll tie these flowers with them—but there, it is not stable enough; let me wrap them with a bit of ribbon, pale blue, from that little dress I wore last winter to the dance, when we had such a long sweet talk in that forgotten nook. (pages 13–15)*

The brief story immediately leaps ahead to Easter some years later to what is presumably the same young lady, now dead for reasons the reader never learns: "Cold, pale, still, its fair young face pressed against the satin-lined casket. Slender, white fingers, idle now, that had never known rest; locked softly over a bunch of violets" (page 16).

There is a leap at this point—in geography, not time—to "a distant city" where a man looking through some old papers "turned over a faded bunch of flowers tied with a blue ribbon and a lock of hair." To his question about whether she had sent the flowers to him, his "regal-looking" wife answers coldly: "You know very well I can't bear flowers. How could I ever send such sentimental trash to anyone? Throw them into the fire" (pages 16–17). Mrs.

Dunbar-Nelson's moral is obvious, and the story, like most of that period, is heavily sentimental: A man should marry a sensitive girl who loves him rather than a wealthy woman who, in her haughtiness, can never give him "true" love. Sentimental or not, however, the story offers close attention to descriptive detail.

The jilted-woman theme is common in Mrs. Dunbar-Nelson's fiction, although "A Story of Vengeance" presents a somewhat unusual approach to the issue, with the abandoned woman exhibiting a kind of female assertiveness, in revenge, not commonly found in the fiction of the time. The story opens with the conversation of two women, the narrator and Eleanor, with the narrator saying: "Why did I never marry? . . . Oh, that's a long story. I'll tell you if you wish; it might pass an hour" (page 98). She once loved, it seems, a man named Bernard, with whom she "had five months of happiness" (page 100) following Bernard's break-off of a love affair with a wealthy woman named Blanche. After the five months, however, Bernard renewed his relationship with Blanche and the narrator was forgotten—but the narrator by no means forgot him:

> *But, mind you, Eleanor, I schemed well. I had everything seemingly that humanity craved for, but I suffered, and by all the gods, I swore that he should suffer too. Blanche turned against him and married his brother. An unfortunate chain of circumstances drove him from his father's home branded as a forger. Strange, wasn't it? But money is a strong weapon, and its long arm reaches over leagues and leagues of land and water. (page 103)*

Having secretly ruined Bernard's life, the narrator later meets Bernard, who pleads with her for an opportunity to renew the relationship. Not content with the secret knowledge of her revenge, the narrator says: "I laughed at him and sneered at his misery, and told him what he had done for my happiness, and what I in turn had done for his" (page 104). Following the revelation, Bernard, "with one awful, indescribable look of hate, anguish and scorn, walked from the room"—just as the narrator felt "all the old love [rising] in me like a flood, drowning the sorrows of past years" (page 104). But it is too late; and after describing herself as "a miserable, heartweary wreck," the narrator closes the story with its moral: "Vengeance is an arrow that often falleth and smiteth the hand of him that sent it" (page 105). A certain tension operates in this story, as the female narrator finds herself in the somewhat uncomfortable role of schemer and "power-broker" in her destruction of her lover's career, love relationship, and life generally.

Another jilted-woman story, though one with a significantly different tone from that of "A Story of Vengeance," is "Little Miss Sophie" (which, incidentally, along with "A Carnival Jangle" and "Titee," also appears in the second collection, *The Goodness of St. Rocque and Other Stories* [5]). It is about a young seamstress living in the "sordid" and "barren" Third District of New Orleans who, while in church one day, recognizes her old lover as a member of a wedding party filing into the church for a marriage. Coincidentally—and coincidence plays a large role in Mrs. Dunbar-Nelson's fiction, as indeed it does in much that was written in nineteenth-century America—Sophie later overhears some men talking aboard a streetcar:

> *"Yes, it's too bad for Neale, and lately married too,"* said the elder man. *"I can't see what he is to do."*
> *Neale! she pricked up her ears. That was the name of the groom in the Jesuit church.*

Sophie listens further, and learns that Neale's company has failed but that he was at first unconcerned, since he was expecting an inheritance from his uncle. But then, Sophie overhears, "this difficulty of identification springs up, and he is literally on the verge of ruin." It seems that the uncle's will stipulates that the heir "shall be known only by a certain quaint Roman ring, and unless he has it—no identification, no fortune."

What has happened to the ring? "He has given the ring away and that settles it" (pages 143–45).

Perhaps predictably enough, Sophie is the one to whom Louis Neale gave the Roman ring that can now insure his fortune, but Sophie had pawned the ring some time before to supply herself with food (never, of course, for personal luxury). She could presumably get from Neale the money to reclaim the ring, but such a direct act is only occasionally used by Mrs. Dunbar-Nelson's characters. Instead Sophie—certainly more in the conventional mode than the assertive narrator in "A Story of Vengeance"—vows that she will work even harder at her sewing and will reclaim the ring and return it to Neale secretly. "The bundle [of sewing] grew larger each day, and Miss Sophie grew smaller. The damp, cold rain and mist closed the white-curtained window, but always there behind the sewing machine drooped and bobbed the little black-robed figure" (page 148).

Miss Sophie is, of course, working herself literally to death. By Christmas she has earned enough to reclaim the ring from the pawnbroker; she does reclaim the ring, and she brings it home for one last night's possession before returning it to Neale the next day. On Christmas morning, Sophie's landlady enters the room to find, first a note, and then Miss Sophie:

> "*Louis. Here is the ring. I return it to you. I heard you needed it, I hope it comes not too late. Sophie.*"

> *"The ring, where?" muttered the landlady. There it was, clasped between her fingers on her bosom. A bosom, white and cold, under a cold, happy face. Christmas had indeed dawned for Miss Sophie—the eternal Christmas. (page 153)*

Here we have a character of quiet heroism, one who might be considered by the somewhat callous standards of the late twentieth century to be a bit mawkish, but one who, in a nearly Christlike way (and I certainly do not wish to press the point), can be made to suffer but can subsequently give up her life trying to redeem the one who has caused her suffering.

Another story of quietly tragic heroism—one that also could, by contemporary emotional standards, be considered mawkish—is "Titee," a story about a young boy living in a poor section of New Orleans who is looked upon by his mother, his teacher, and others as "idle, lazy, dirty, [and] troublesome" (page 212). "But there was nothing in natural history that Titee didn't know. He could dissect a butterfly or a mosquito-hawk and describe their parts as accurately as a spectacled student with a scalpel and microscope could talk about a cadaver" (pages 212–213). Titee suddenly develops the habits of taking most of his breakfast with him when he leaves the house in the morning, of arriving at school late each day, and of having no lunch with him when he does arrive.

One day Titee does not come home at night. A search party is formed and begins its search in a violent rainstorm for the young boy. "And then, after awhile they found a pitiful little heap of wet and sodden rags, laying at the foot of a mound of earth and stones thrown upon the side of the track. It was little Titee with a broken leg" (page 221). Titee, still not concerned about himself, directs the search party to a nearby cave, and then everyone understands Titee's secret.

> *In one of his trips around the swampland, he had discovered the old man exhausted from cold and hunger in the fields. Together they had found this cave, and Titee had gathered the straw [that] made the bed. . . . And thither Titee had trudged twice a day, carrying his luncheon in the morning, and his dinner in the afternoon.*
>
> *"There's a crown in Heaven for that child," said the officer of charity to whom the case was referred. (pages 223–24)*

Again, the device is melodramatic and the moral almost too apparent. The device is that of secretly doing good while outwardly appearing irresponsible, so that when the good deeds are found out, the judges (in this case, the mother, teacher, and community generally) will feel remorse for their misjudgments. The moral is for no person to judge the actions of another without knowing what is "in his heart." And, again, the point is made that sacrificing to help those less well-off is, after all, a rather noble thing to do.

Perhaps because of the tendency toward melodrama, the few critical judgments that have been made about the stories originally published in *Violets* have been mixed. Vernon Loggins, on the negative side, calls the collection one of those "things which most authors who ever do anything better would like to destroy" (6). On the other hand, *Violets* was quite favorably reviewed in the Boston *Daily Standard* (7). Paul Laurence Dunbar (not an altogether objective critic even at this point in their relationship, we must acknowledge), in a letter to the then Miss Moore, said about *Violets*: ". . . since I have seen your book, I am fairly bewildered. I have read it with delight, and my appreciation is equalled only by my surprise. . . . I consider your stories pieces of most exquisite art. . . . Your 'Little Miss

Sophie' is as graceful, poignant and charming as anything Grace King ever wrote" (8).

The most interesting story found in *Violets*—perhaps because it is the most original as well as the one that most reflects the author's strong commitment to women's rights—is "The Woman," an interior monologue of the narrator on the question, "Why should well-salaried women marry?" In arguments and language remarkably like those of the 1980s, the narrator outlines the advantages that a single woman has over a typical wife and mother.

To begin with, once her day's work is finished, the single woman goes home, often to a boarding-house where her meals are prepared for her. She has no household cares, no dinners to prepare; no "fault-finding husband" and "no fretful children." Of course, she has debts and scrimpings, but overall she has a great deal of freedom.

> *She does not incessantly rely upon the whims of a cross man to take her to such amusements as she desires. In this nineteenth century she is free to go where she pleases—provided it be in a moral atmosphere—without comment. Theatres, concerts, lectures, and the lighter amusements of social affairs among her associates, are open to her, and there she can go, see, and be seen, admire and be admired, enjoy and be enjoyed, without a single harrowing thought of the baby's milk or the husband's coffee. (pages 22–23)*

The woman's life, says the narrator, is one of financial independence: her earnings are her own. She has geographical independence, traveling where she pleases in the summer. Moreover she has intellectual independence, her mind broadened by contact with the world, and "in her leisure moments by the better thoughts of dead and living men which she meets in her applications to books and periodicals; in her vacations, by her studies of nature, or it may be other communities than her own" (page 24). Finally, she has sexual independence: "Marriages might be made in Heaven, but too often they are consummated right here on earth, based on a desire to possess the physical attractions of the woman by the man" (pages 25–26).

The narrator concludes her monologue with an answer to "conservative" responses to her claims:

> *"They say" that men don't admire this type of woman, that they prefer the soft, dainty, winning, mindless creature who cuddles into men's arms, agrees to everything they say, and looks upon them as a race of gods turned loose upon this earth for the edification of womankind. Well, may be so, but there is one thing positive, they certainly respect the independent one, and admire her, too, even if it is at a distance, and that in itself is something. (page 27)*

Mrs. Dunbar-Nelson's best-rendered ethnic portraits—especially those of New Orleans Creoles, although some concentrate, quite negatively as a rule, on Italians and the Irish—are found in her second collection of stories, *The Goodness of St. Rocque and Other Stories*. Vernon Loggins, who was flatly negative in his comments about *Violets*, says the collection "has some excellent material handled with pleasing effect" (9). Paul Laurence Dunbar goes further:

> *Your determination to contest Cable for his laurels is a commendable one. Why shouldn't you tell those pretty Creole stories as well as he? You have the force, the fire and the artistic touch that is so delicate and yet so strong.*
>
> *Do you know that New Orleans—in fact all of Louisiana seems to me to be a kind of romance land? Its*

> *very atmosphere must teem with stories and its streets and by-ways be redolent of dramatic incident that lingers as a sort of perfume from a fragrant past. No wonder you have Grace King and Geo. W. Cable, no wonder you will have Alice R. M. (10).*

The title story, "The Goodness of Saint Rocque," a fine example of Dunbar-Nelson's excellent description and dialect, features a New Orleans Creole girl named Manuela, who, fearing that she is losing her lover to another woman, secretly consults a fortune teller, who shuffles her cards "in her long grimy talons" (page 8). She reports that, although the lover is interested in another, the use of a charm and prayers to St. Rocque may redirect his love toward Manuela:

> *"I give you one lil' charm, yaas," said the Wizened One when the seance was over, and Manuela, all white and nervous, leaned back in the rickety chair. "I give you one lil' charm fo' to ween him back, yaas. You wear h'it 'roun' you' wais', an' he come back. Den you mek prayer at St. Rocque an' burn can'le. Den you come back an' tell me, yaas. Cinquante sous, ma'amzelle. Merci. Good luck go wid you." (page 9)*

Manuela performs the necessary rituals, and, sure enough, Theophile begins to pay her court once more, much to the dismay of the hopeful Claralie. There is little more to the story, except the closing observation that St. Rocque "is a good saint, and if you believe in him and are true and good, and make your novenas with a clean heart, he will grant your wish" (page 16)

The story does reveal, however, Mrs. Dunbar-Nelson's interest in ethnic portraits (almost stereotypes at times), in this instance such inclusive observations about Creoles as "your true Creole never leaves the small folks at home" (page 4); and "For your Creole girls are proud, and would die rather than let the world see their sorrows" (page 13); and "Now you know, when a Creole young man places a girl at his mother's right hand at his own table, there is but one conclusion to be deduced therefrom" (pages 15–16). In his book *Black New Orleans 1860–1880,* incidentally, John Blassingame lists Alice Dunbar-Nelson, along with Rodolph Desdunes, Charles Rousseve, Ernest J. Gaines, and several others, as continuing the New Orleans Creole of color tradition in literature, a tradition that began during Reconstruction (11).

The most outstanding stories of Mrs. Dunbar-Nelson's second collection are "M'sieu Fortier's Violin" and "Mr. Baptiste," both sensitive portrayals of the misfortunes of old men. M'sieu Fortier is a concert violinist who "had played first violin in the orchestra ever since—well, no one remembered his not playing there" (page 70). One day, however, M'sieu Fortier learns that the opera house where he has played so many years has been sold and that the new conductor is a talented, progressive, and energetic young man. M'sieu Fortier accepts $50 that is offered for his violin by a long-term admirer of the instrument. Six days later, M'sieu Fortier arrives at the home of Courcey, the man who bought the violin, to say:

> *"I come fo' bring back you' money, yaas. I cannot sleep. I cannot eat, I only cry, and t'ink, and weesh fo' mon violon; and Minesse, an' de ol' woman too, dey mope an' look bad too, all for mon violon. I try fo' to use dat money, but eeet burn an' sting lak blood money. I feel lak' I don sol' my child. I cannot go a l'opera no mo', I t'ink of mon violon. I starve befo' I live widout. My heart, he is broke, I die for mon violon." (page 82)*

Courcey immediately returns the violin, saying: "as for the money, why, keep that too; it was worth a hundred dollars to have possessed such an instrument even for six days" (page 82). Although a warmly rendered sketch of Creole life, the problem is that, despite the story's warmth and charm, it has no resolution. M'sieu Fortier remains impoverished, and the cherished violin seems unlikely to do anything to remedy that situation.

The protagonist of "Mr. Baptiste" "was small: most Creole men are small when they are old. It is strange, but a fact" (page 111). Mr. Baptiste "subsisted by doing odd jobs, whitewashing, cleaning yards, doing errands and the like" (page 112). Also Mr. Baptiste spends much of his free time at the New Orleans docks watching the cotton and fruit being loaded and unloaded by the longshoremen. The only racial reference in the book (although the ethnic references, even in this story, are frequent) begins when the excited Mr. Baptiste tells a friend that "dose 'longsho'mans, dey go out on one strik'. Dey t'row down dey tool an' say dey work no mo' wid niggers." (page 115).

Soon the battle lines on the dock are drawn, with the mostly Irish longshoremen (their leader is Finnegan) on one side, and the Blacks, who are continuing to work despite the strike, on the other.

> "Niggers!" *roared Finnegan wrathily.*
> "Niggers! niggers! Kill 'em, scabs!" *chorused the crowd.*
> *With muscles standing out like cables through their blue cotton shirts, and sweat rolling from glossy black skins, the Negro stevedores were at work steadily labouring at the cotton, with the rhythmic song swinging its cadence in the hot air. The roar of the crowd caused the men to look up with momentary apprehension, but at the overseer's reassuring word they bent back to work.*

> *Finnegan was a Titan. With livid face and bursting veins he ran into the street facing the French Market, and uprooted a huge block of paving stone. Staggering under its weight, he rushed back to the ship, and with one mighty effort hurled it into the hold.*
>
> *The delicate poles of the costly machine tottered in the air, then fell forward with a crash as the whole iron framework in the hold collapsed.*
>
> *"Damn ye," shouted Finnegan, "now yez can pack yer cotton!" (pages 120–21)*

Soon the Blacks begin returning bricks, pieces of iron, and pieces of wood; and after one particularly good volley, Mr. Baptiste, who is watching from behind a bread-stall, cheers. Hearing him, one of the Irish longshoremen, McMahon, roars: "Cheerin' the niggers, are you?" and "he let fly a brickbat in the direction of the bread-stall," after which "Mr. Baptiste lay very still, with a great ugly gash in his wrinkled brown temple" (page 122).

Aside from the doctor's flat statement, "Killed instantly" (page 123), there is little left for the reader to assume except something about the racial bigotry and hostility of workmen of Irish extraction. And this brings us to another interesting point about Mrs. Dunbar-Nelson's ethnic portraits: her negative treatment—certainly in keeping with common attitudes in New Orleans at the time—of the "lower order" of immigrants, especially the Irish (as in the characters Finnegan and McMahon) and the Italians, as in "Tony's Wife."

"Tony's Wife" is a familiar nineteenth-century story about a cruel and drunken husband (of Italian extraction, it is carefully pointed out) and a suffering and forbearing "wife," who "was meek, pale, little, ugly, and German" (page 23). Tony is introduced as "a low growl," as "beetle-browed and huge" (page 19). Tony and his "wife" own a small grocery shop on Prytania Street in New Orleans, where the long-battered "wife" spends her days selling small items, knitting, and being badgered by her husband ("'Hurry up there, will you?' growled the black brows" [pages 20–21]). The reader presumably is to gather that Tony's cruelty is the direct result of his Italian ancestry:

> *He was a great, black-bearded, hoarse-voiced, six-foot specimen of Italian humanity, who looked in his little shop and on the prosaic pavement of Prytania Street somewhat as Hercules might seem in a modern drawing-room. You instinctively thought of wild mountain-passes, and the gleaming dirks of bandit contadini in looking at him. (page 22)*

The story is mainly, in fact, a catalog of the man's viciousness: "When she displeased him, he beat her, and knocked her frail form on the floor" (page 25); and "[The wife's] mother appeared upon the scene once, and stayed a short time; but Tony got drunk one day and beat her because she ate too much, and she disappeared soon after" (page 25). One day Tony falls ill; and after his examination, the doctor announces to the "wife" that her husband, apparently because of his evil ways, "is completely burned out inside. Empty as a shell. . . . He cannot live, for he has nothing to live on" (page 28).

It is here that the reader learns that Tony and his "wife" are not married after all, for just before Tony's death, the woman who suffers so eagerly pleads with him. However, consistent with his almost tediously evil character, Tony refuses to marry the woman; and so, when he dies, his property goes to his brother. And "as for Tony's wife, since she was not his wife after all, they sent her forth in the world penniless, her worn fingers clutching her bundle of clothes" (page 33). Other drunkards appear in nineteenth-century fiction and poetry, particularly in the numerous temperance novels, but interestingly, unlike virtually all of those other drunkards, the source of Tony's evil temperament is not alcohol but heritage. Put simply: he is Italian.

Alice Dunbar-Nelson's literary achievements are; to be sure, somewhat modest ones. The issues in her stories—and some of the pieces are, in fact, sketches—do not always have substantial depth, and some seem designed for quick dramatic impact that might have been provided a bit more legitimately with somewhat slower working out of plot. But for all of that, those who call her stories of New Orleans charming, with careful detail and good dialect, and with an accurate capturing of ethnic rituals (and prejudices), are quite right. And although she has remained almost completely unknown, she has deserved better.

NOTES

1. Eugene Wesley Metcalf, *The Letters of Paul and Alice Dunbar: A Private History*. Diss., University of California, Irvine, 1973), xxxii.
2. Metcalf, 2.
3. Metcalf, 4.
4. Alice Ruth Moore, *Violets and Other Tales* (Boston: The Monthly Review Press, 1895), 5; all page references are to this edition.
5. *St. Rocque* was originally published in New York by Dodd, Mead in 1899. All page references to stories in the volume are made to the McGrath reprint published in College Park, Maryland, in 1969.
6. Vernon Loggins, *The Negro Author, His Development in America to 1900* (New York: Columbia University Press, 1964), 318.

7. Metcalf, 65.
8. Metcalf, 63.
9. Loggins, 318.
10. Metcalf, 80.
11. John W. Blassingame, *Black New Orleans 1860–1880* (Chicago: University of Chicago Press, 1973), 137.

V

Psychology, Religion, and Regionalism

Chapter 7

Geography as Psychology in the Writings of Margaret Laurence

By Cathy N. Davidson

In the Canadian fiction of Margaret Laurence, geography is close to destiny. And destiny, for each of this author's five protagonists, begins with and is substantially determined by a mythic prairie town. The physical, psychological, and social landscape of that town—Manawaka, Manitoba—pervades the lives of those who have lived there. Thus, it is not surprising that only one novel, *A Jest of God* (1966), is set completely in Manawaka. Characters depart yet eventually discover that at least in memory they must go home again. Indeed, in Laurence's four other major Canadian works (three novels and one collection of related short stories), a woman finds that only by trying to discover the meaning of her past can she begin to understand the reality of her present. Previous events and present awareness remain inextricably bound. In other words, inner and outer landscapes merge into each other, and even Manawaka itself becomes as much a state of mind as a place on a map. But by recognizing the complex interrelationship of geography and psychology, Laurence's characters survive and a few even manage to achieve art.

Manawaka, however, never becomes merely a metaphor for some character's mental state. Laurence repeatedly stresses the physical reality of the place—a varied but not dramatic town situated on a river that flows among gently rolling, still partly wooded hills (1). The town's sociological divisions correspond, moreover, to its geographical ones. The natural features of the scene seem to divide the wealthy Scottish families from the impoverished Métis, and to separate both from the Ukrainian farmers who, four generations after their arrival, are still seen as immigrants not fully incorporated into the life of the province. In fact, Manawakan topography partly recapitulates world ethnogeography. Yet, paradoxically, this geography also can be seen as substantially mental. Since each ethnic group has definite fixed ideas about its own virtues and others' vices, nationality (that is, place of birth, even in one particular town) partly determines psychology. Growing up in Manawaka entails the acquisition of a certain set of ethnic definitions.

But further growth requires that one come to terms with one's past. That task is always difficult. It is especially so, as Rachel Cameron in *A Jest of God* finds out, when previously inculcated codes and values must be questioned. And in her case, as her situation at the beginning of the novel attests, the ethos she lives by surely merits critical scrutiny. She feels that she is trapped in the middle-class mores insisted upon by the Scotch Presbyterians of Manawaka, that she is manipulated by her mother's self-serving rhetoric of righteousness and respectability. Yet even though she seems to understand Mrs. Cameron's obviously selfish tactics and apparently recognizes the sterility of the general moral code that the mother effectively represents, Rachel still cannot acknowledge—and thus have some basis for reacting against—a heritage that demands her continual self-denial and self-effacement.

Her only defense has been evasion. Like her late father, Rachel usually resists by withdrawing. An undertaker, Niall Cameron eluded the claims of respectability by getting drunk among the corpses. Rachel too endures a kind of living death: she ages but does not grow. Instead, she has marked time since she returned to Manawaka, after one year of college, in order to support the widowed Mrs. Cameron. For some 14 years she has been treated as if she were an adolescent who required a mother's rules and regulations, and she still inhabits the frilled and ruffled bedroom of a virginal young girl. In short, at 34, Rachel is entering middle age without having reached her majority.

Trapped by the mores of the town, Rachel is also a victim of her own apprehensions. We can note, for example, her fear that she might become the stereotypical "old maid schoolteacher." This reaction really represents the fear of appearing eccentric. Rachel is herself unwilling to abandon accepted standards, to seem foolish. As she at one point observes: "I can't bear scenes. They make me ill" (2). Mrs. Cameron could well have said the same thing. Too afraid that she might be unfavorably noticed, the daughter allows her life to fall into the monotonous and repetitious pattern prescribed by small-town notions of propriety.

There are, however, numerous hints that Rachel will not remain as she is at the beginning of the novel. Even the narrative technique Laurence employs shows that behind the facade of the respectable spinster there is another Rachel, an intellectually curious and emotionally passionate woman. Much of the novel, in fact, consists of a debate between these two faces of Rachel. One aspect of the daughter advocates, as just noted, the values espoused by her mother and the code insisted upon by middle-class Manawaka. But this voice never silences another voice that speaks for individual freedom and personal fulfillment. The resulting impasse obviously cannot last.

Typically, Rachel first attempts to circumvent through external means the role that the town and the internalized values of the town prescribe for her. She has an affair with Nick Kazlik. This former resident, also a teacher, knows Manawaka well enough to understand Rachel's predicament. But as a Ukrainian, he has never himself been restricted by the Calvinistic morality against which Rachel finally rebels. Nevertheless, Nick has not himself fully escaped from his own Manawaka. He still reluctantly spends an occasional summer on the farm to which his father wishes he would permanently return. Of course, Rachel is too bound up with her own dilemmas to recognize that he can hardly serve as her savior. Their relationship, on most levels, is unsuccessful and emphasizes a pervasive theme in Laurence's writings, that one person cannot save another. As Rachel can recognize only retrospectively, Nick all along had his "own demons and webs" (page 189).

Still Rachel requires the affair, and by having it succeeds in opening some doors (3). Both symbolically and psychologically, her relationship with Nick marks her first departure from the morality she formerly half-heartedly upheld. She discovers that she can run the risk of appearing foolish, that she is willing to take chances. Furthermore, by making herself vulnerable to pain and rejection, she also learns something about herself. She finds that she needs to love and be loved, that she is not satisfied with her present life, and that there are things she can do to change it.

One thing she must do is leave Manawaka. The longer she remains in the town, the more she becomes a part of it, another feature of the landscape. The affair with Nick is a first step toward defining her own identity. She takes a second step when she decides to move to British Columbia. Leaving Manawaka, however, is by no means synonymous with personal salvation. The final pages of the novel make clear the extent to which Rachel has achieved, to use Laurence's phrase, "a limited victory" (4). On the one hand, she will not change dramatically: "I will grow too orderly.... I will be afraid" (page 202). But even though she must accept fundamental aspects of her own nature, she still can partly direct the course her life should follow. For example, given her personality and her sense of responsibility, she cannot abandon her mother. Yet neither can she abandon herself. When she dropped out of college to support her mother, she too readily acquiesced to that situation and accepted it as an inevitable (although often lamented) fate. After the affair, however, she belatedly sees that she need not continue to play the role of the child. "I am the mother now," she finally, and with considerable justification, insists (page 184),

But maturity is not achieved simply by relocating in Vancouver. Rachel will discover, as do other Laurence characters, that physical departure from Manawaka does not necessarily mean concomitant psychological escape from the town's influence. Hagar Shipley, for example, moves from Manawaka to Vancouver long before Rachel does. Intending independence, she thinks she has left behind her both her husband and the memory of her father. Yet Hagar, the nonagenarian protagonist of *The Stone Angel* (1964), finds that her life continues to be haunted by the ghosts of her past.

Stacey Cameron MacAindra, Rachel's older sister, has made the same journey. She left home at eighteen. But in *The Fire-Dwellers* (1969), we see that, some 20 years later, Stacey confronts in Vancouver the same problems her sister in Manawaka faced. The novels *A Jest of God* and *The Fire-Dwellers* should, in fact, be read together (5). Rachel, in the first of these two works, believes that the sister who has left Manawaka and who has a family of her own must be happy. In the second, however, we see that Rachel's envy is definitely naïve. Like Rachel, Stacey fears that she is "spending [her] life in one unbroken series of trivialities" (6). Like Rachel, she fights against too much resembling her parents, and yet she frequently hears herself repeating their words. She too must come to terms with her past. She is continually taken back into that past by some present experience. Yet these continuing encounters finally bring her to accept herself as an adult:

> *I used to think there would be a blinding flash of light someday, and then I would be wise and calm and would know how to cope with everything and my kids would rise up and call me blessed. Now I see that whatever I'm like, I'm pretty well stuck with it for life. Hell of a revelation that turned out to be. (7)*

But the revelation does reconcile her to her previous life in the provincial town, to her present life in the coastal city. And Vancouver, it should be noted, does not function in Laurence's fiction simply as a Canadian Florida, a place to get away from it all. *The Fire-Dwellers* includes the death of a would-be lover, the attempted suicide of a close friend, and the near-drowning of a son—showing that Vancouver, despite its mild climate and urban amenities, has its dark underside (8). And it too can foster the same awareness that Manawaka does. In both, place and personality interact. The character who can appreciate the diversity, the multiplicity, inherent in a community that is (or was) the setting for her life more fully comprehends the complexity of her life, too. Stacey better understands—and therefore accepts—herself after she has come to terms with her past, with the Manawaka that shaped that self.

The remaining two works in the Manawaka series, *A Bird in the House* (1970) and *The Diviners* (1974), examine essentially the same problem but do so from a rather different point of view. Each of these books centers on a protagonist who is a writer. Both, therefore, address more explicitly and philosophically the question of how one's past informs one's present. Again, the past is primarily Manawaka and, at first, a burden that must be shed. Thus Vanessa MacLeod, whose retrospectively related stories of her children comprise *A Bird in the House,* early wished to escape the scene of that childhood. But she also comes to see that Manawaka, for all its small-minded restrictiveness, must be generously assessed, for the town provides her with both the vision and material that shape her art.

One story particularly exemplifies the processes whereby Vanessa achieves her adult perspective. This tale, "Mask of the Bear," begins with the young would-be author attempting to compose a romance of ancient Egypt. Her subject requires, she believes, such a distant setting: "Both death and love seemed regrettably far from Manawaka" (9). Soon, however, she realizes that despite a concern for propriety, which requires that emotions be denied or repressed, Manawaka has its tragedies and passions. Her Grandmother Connor dies and her Aunt Edna's love affair ends abortively. Vanessa, an inveterate listener at keyholes, catches hints of how much each event means even to those who feign indifference. She experiences an epiphany that prompts her to revaluate the lives of those she thought she knew.

Incidentally, she also destroys the story she was writing. Later she will carry the process of revaluation even further. Rather than abandoning a wildly romantic tale, she will complete a real one. The composing of this final story, and the content of the story, demonstrate the possibilities for life and art in Manawaka—possibilities made, if anything, more valuable by not being immediately obvious.

But it is *The Diviners*, the last book in the Manawaka series, that perhaps best represents Laurence's subtle illustration of how complex the examined simple life can be. Morag Gunn, the protagonist in that novel, persistently revaluates her memories and the meanings of those memories, even recalling at what point in the process she invented certain events or specific interpretations of imaginary or actual occurrences. Characteristically, she early confesses that she keeps her "snapshots not for what they show, but for what is hidden in them" (10). Despite her early flight first to college and the closest city, then to marriage and Toronto, then from marriage to Vancouver, and even to exile in England, she still remains emotionally tied to the Manitoba town. In fact, as the novel makes clear, she leaves Manawaka partly in order to encounter it. One reason for living in England and visiting Scotland is to discover her own ancestral roots. As Morag herself recognizes, the place she finally chooses to live, McConnell's Landing, is an Ontario version of Manawaka. Here too she lives tangentially to the town, still an outsider and somewhat suspect.

And just as Morag's present partly reproduces her past (McConnell's Landing as Manawaka), so too do the events in that present partly recapitulate the past. When *The Diviners* opens, Morag Gunn is 47 years old; her daughter, Pique, is 18. Illegitimate and part Indian, Pique is as much an outsider as was Morag, the orphan taken in by Manawaka's garbage collector. There are other parallels, too. Early in the summer Pique leaves home. Even though the mother at the same age acted the same way, she worries constantly until her daughter returns. But Morag is more sympathetic when her daughter is ready to leave again. By the end of the summer, she can better understand the other's desire for individual freedom. Furthermore, because Pique wishes to go live with her Uncle Jacques, the one member of her father's family who survives, Morag sees that the daughter too is searching for her past in order to understand her present. Significantly, in coming to terms with her daughter's departure, Morag is doing on a symbolic and psychological level exactly the same thing that Pique does. In the course of the summer (and the course of the novel), Morag recounts her past life. She looks for patterns, for divinations, that will allow her to understand her daughter's need for individuality and her own early and continuing similar demand.

Morag realizes that she is not her daughter, that Pique is not Morag. Yet Pique must leave McConnell's Landing just as Morag, like Laurence's other protagonists, had to leave Manawaka. Leaving, Pique takes with her the songs that her father has written about his past; Morag is sure Pique will some day write songs about her father, the songs he could never write about himself. And as the book ends, Morag herself sits down to write the title of her next novel, a novel that derives from her own life, from the lived and relived past. Here too the work validates its author's Manawaka experience and subsequent life. Again, geography becomes psychology and both, as in *A Bird in the House*, are then transmuted into art.

NOTES

1. Laurence R. Ricou, in "Empty as Nightmare: Man and Landscape in Recent Canadian Prairie Fiction," *Mosaic* 6:2 (1973), 143–60, emphasizes that Manawaka sits only on the edge of the prairies. It lacks the uninterrupted flatness that makes the prairie land-

scape a "perfect metaphor for existential, universal meaninglessness" (148).
2. Margaret Laurence, *A Jest of God* (Toronto: McClelland and Stewart, 1966), 46; all page references to this edition.
3. Speaking of the main characters in her fiction, Margaret Laurence has said: "A great many things that have to do with personal liberation or freedom, it seems to me, involve labouring mightily against a door which actually is not locked." See Graeme Gibson, ed., *Eleven Canadian Novelists* (Toronto: Anansi Press, 1973), 206.
4. Quoted in Gibson, 204.
5. Clara Thomas, in *The Manawaka World of Margaret Laurence* (Toronto: McClelland and Stewart, 1976), 131, notes that "Margaret Laurence has said that she would like the five Manawaka works to be read, essentially, as one work."
6. Margaret Laurence, *The Fire-Dwellers* (Toronto: McClelland and Stewart, 1969), 95.
7. Laurence, *The Fire-Dwellers,* 298–99.
8. Clara Thomas compares the Vancouver of *The Fire-Dwellers* to "a vast canvas by Hieronymus Bosch whose every corner is filled with devilish manifestations of aberration, cruelty, and desperation, and the whole lit with hellish flames" *(The Manawaka World of Margaret Laurence,* 188).
9. Margaret Laurence, *A Bird in the House* (Toronto: McClelland and Stewart, 1970), 65.
10. Margaret Laurence, *The Diviners* (Toronto: Bantam Books, 1974), 6.

Chapter 8

Women Regionalists of Mormon Country

By Edward A. Geary

"Mormon Country" is largely a state of mind but also a geographical reality including Utah and sizable parts of Idaho, Wyoming, and Arizona, with scattered outposts as far from the center as Canada and Mexico. The Mormons came to this region in the mid-nineteenth century as refugees in search of a place where they could develop their own culture and practice their own beliefs (including, but not limited to, plural marriage) without interference. They did not succeed in escaping the dominant American society, but for 50 years they held it at bay, resisting attempts to "Americanize" them. It was during this period of isolation (and of persecution that solidified group-feeling and sharpened the sense of being a peculiar people) that Mormon Country took shape. It is a shape sufficiently distinctive that geographers speak of "the Mormon landscape" and sociologists and anthropologists of "the Mormon village."

These would seem to be conditions that would stimulate development of a regional literature, especially when one considers that Mormonism began with a book and that the early leaders of the church were fascinated with language—Brigham Young going so far as to promote the "Desert Alphabet," an effort at phonetic spelling reform. And yet an authentic regional literature was slow to develop. Most Mormon writing aimed at a wider audience has been polemical: attacks or exposés by those outside the church, apologies or missionary tracts by those within—in either case presenting a distorted view of Mormon life.

The so-called "home literature" produced for the Mormon audience in the nineteenth and early twentieth centuries was merely an adaptation of the formulas of genteel popular fiction and verse, a simple-minded combination of didacticism and sentimentality. The 1920s and '30s saw a few attempts at more serious work. As late as 1938, however, Bernard DeVoto (himself a product of Mormon Country, though never a Mormon) was predicting failure for anyone who tried "to compose fiction out of Joseph Smith and the Mormon people." He declared that "God, the best story-teller, has made a better story out of Joseph and the Mormon wandering than fiction will ever equal" and called his own Mormon novel "the best book I am never going to write" (1). The following year Vardis Fisher's Harper Prize novel *Children of God: An American Epic* appeared, and Mormon regional fiction came into being.

Of the Mormon writers who published novels during the next several years, the majority were women, including the two who seem to me the most interesting, Maurine Whipple and Virginia Sorensen (2). But whether women or men, they nearly all belonged to a single generation. They were born in the first two decades of the twentieth century, at the end of the era of isolation yet at a time when many of the pioneer generation still survived to tell the stories of early-day hardships. Many of them participated in the out-migration from Mormon Country that took place between 1920 and 1950, leaving their native province for California or the East. Yet like many other provincial peoples, they were unable to break loose from their roots, and most of their fiction represents an effort to come to terms with their Mormon heritage.

Their novels are seldom set in a period later than their own childhood and tend to be nostalgic, a celebration of a more heroic age and a lament at its passing. This is not an uncommon pattern in regional literature. Wallace Stegner (another non-Mormon from Mormon Country) has suggested that most Western regional writers feel "a common impotence when we step outside our own myth, or outside the history that has been suspended ever since our boyhood. We cannot find, apparently, a present and living society that is truly ours and that contains the materials of a deep commitment" (3).

Both Maurine Whipple and Virginia Sorensen have acknowledged the regional quality in themselves and their work. Whipple claims to have had the idea for *The Giant Joshua* "as long as I could remember." Speaking of the period when she was writing the novel, she says, "Some of the old people were alive then—Uncle Charlie Seegmiller was 95, Aunt Jane Blake was 90 something—and I just went and talked to them. I got so immersed in that era—reading everything and wandering the hills and sitting upon the red hills and visualizing everything—that it was almost as if I had lived through it myself" (4).

Virginia Sorensen has similarly expressed her sense that she carries the regional past with her, whether she wishes to or not. She too describes a conversation with an old woman who had lived the pioneer experience and who spoke of people and events long past as though they were still living and present. *"It is as if they were all here.* This is the feeling of Utah that I carry helplessly with me, also, though I have lived much less of its history than has this wonderful old woman. I too have a deep consciousness about the so-immediate and yet so-remote past of town after town, valley after valley. Our history here and our legends are so close to us that it is all but impossible to separate ourselves from them" (5).

Yet Sorensen also realizes that there are limitations in this regional orientation. "The fact is that mere quaintness and color are no longer of much importance in the kind of world we now live in," she says (page 283). "If regionalism has ceased to be important, then what is our dilemma as writers who find it essential, and all writers must, to create out of our own background and experience? The answer to it, I believe, is that we manage somehow to expand these into the necessary importance by finding their place and meaning in the world at large—I mean that we discover their wider truth" (page 284).

The peculiarities of Mormon Country make that task a challenging one. Probably no other region of the United States, except for early New England, has been so shaped and dominated by a single church, and a church with a passion for organization. The settlement of Mormon Country was communal rather than individualistic. The villages did not simply grow up around a crossroads store; instead, people were "called" on settlement missions and went to the chosen site in a group presided over by the bishop, who was civil leader and magistrate as well as ecclesiastical leader. The villages were usually laid out according to a common pattern, derived from Joseph Smith's "Plat of the City of Zion," with large blocks and wide streets intersecting at right angles, the rigid pattern further emphasized by straight rows of Lombardy poplars planted along the streets.

The communities, then, were highly structured both in plan and in social patterns. People lived in town and commuted out to their fields, reversing the pattern of most of rural America. Communal values took precedence over individual tastes; obedience to authority was more important than individual judgment; and the achieving of communal goals mattered more than personal fulfillment, or rather, personal fulfillment was to be attained through the achieving of communal goals.

This pattern ran throughout the entire territory. Brigham Young was governor of the territory as well as president of the church. Church courts settled everything from violations of the Word of Wisdom to marital disputes to murder. (Perhaps even polygamy was an expression of this Mormon fondness for organization: the family itself became a little kingdom.) Sessions of the territorial legislature resembled church conferences and were sometimes conducted as such. Even after the federal government enforced a formal separation of civil authority from ecclesiastical authority, the overlapping remained extensive. Even today, in Mormon towns, the leading church authorities are likely to be the leading figures in the political and economic life of the community, and church policies and practices are taken for granted in many aspects of community life.

Physical conditions, as well as beliefs, had an important influence on the development of highly structured communities. The semiarid conditions made irrigation imperative for agriculture, and the irrigation works needed were usually too extensive for a single individual or family to develop and maintain. Indeed, the irrigation system is a good symbol for the organization of the Mormon village. When Wallace Stegner gave the title *The Sound of Mountain Water* to his book on what it means to be a Westerner and a Western writer, he was thinking primarily of water running free in mountain streams, a fine symbol of the freedom and openness of the West. But the Mormons (as

Stegner himself points out in *Mormon Country*), did not settle in the mountains but in the valleys. They settled wherever there was a large enough stream flowing from the mountains to support a community, and the Mormon story of the water is not of water running free but of water impounded, water diverted, water flowing slowly in the canals dug by the whole community, then divided into smaller and smaller streams to nourish the fields and gardens of each individual family.

The story of the water carries with it its own peculiar laws and thus its peculiar possibilities for lawlessness. The Water Master, as Virginia Sorensen has said, was "an official of great importance in a Utah town" (6)—a representative of communal values and social order—and the water thief, the individual who put his own needs above the needs of the community, was a threat to the entire social fabric. Sorensen's "Where Nothing Is Long Ago" is the story of the killing of a water thief and its effect upon a Mormon town.

> *"But why did he hit him like that?" Mother asked my father. "It's not like Brother Tolsen to strike anybody. Such a gentle man!"*
>
> *"Twice he had turned Brother Tolsen's water off his fields in the night. Twice!" My father spoke with the patience of a man obliged to explain violence to a woman (pages 7–8).*

Significantly, the murdered water thief is a jack-Mormon (a lapsed or nominal Mormon) and his killer a faithful member of the church. Significantly, too, scarcely anyone in the community disapproves of Brother Tolsen's action. "Brother Tolsen had given up at once to the authorities: first to his Bishop, which was entirely proper in all eyes, and then—in company with Bishop Petersen—to the sheriff" (page 13). He is, of course, acquitted.

The real center of the story, however, is neither Brother Tolsen nor the man he hit in the head with his shovel but the narrator, who is remembering the events from her childhood and who sees in them a key to understanding her own relationship to the community. Even as a child, she is not fully in harmony with community opinion. Several months after the trial, she is out riding with her parents and sees Brother Tolsen tending water in his field:

> *"I wonder if he brought a new shovel," I said suddenly. For a minute, the air seemed to have gone dead about us, in the peculiar way it sometimes can, which is so puzzling to a child. Then Mother turned to me angrily. "Don't you ever let me hear you say a thing like that again!" she said. "Brother Tolsen is a good, kind man!" (page 14).*

This is perhaps that "place and meaning in the world at large" that Sorensen seeks for her regional materials. The writer, she has said, is "'in the middle'—incapable of severe orthodoxies," and is striving "to somehow balance the importance of the individual (his respected and ancient concern) with the importance of the great events that wash people into vast groups and crowds into anonymous armies" (7). When the community has the importance that it has historically possessed in Mormon Country, when obedience is valued above individuality, then the role of the independent-minded individual in the community becomes an interesting and revealing one.

The protagonist in Mormon regional fiction is usually a character "in the middle": something of an individualist yet at the same time involved with church and community, caught between his instinct for freedom and the demands of loyalty and obedience. I should say *her* instinct for freedom, for the protagonists of Maurine Whipple and Virginia Sorensen are nearly always women. The woman's point of view is a good one from which to explore this issue in Mormon regional fiction, because in Mormonism the woman is without authority. She is expected to support the goals of the community, but those goals are formulated by "the priesthood," a body that includes virtually all Mormon men. Many women find, or seem to find, their role satisfactory. However, the woman who does not is likely to experience strong tensions.

Most of Virginia Sorensen's protagonists stand somewhat apart from the community, yet almost never can they entirely pull themselves away. Sorensen's finest novel, *The Evening and the Morning,* deals with three generations of women in a small Mormon town. Kate Alexander has rebelled against the community values, has left the church and moved to Los Angeles, where she has become a social worker and a feminist, yet has come back to Manti, Utah, in an effort to pull together the loose ends of her life. Her daughter Dessie (for Deseret), is trying to be happy in the prescribed role of Mormon wife and mother; and the granddaughter Jean (obviously an autobiographical figure) is a high-strung child with a vivid imagination, encountering the turmoil of early adolescence.

Kate, the central figure in the novel, is a remarkably honest and responsible woman, and a rebel against the narrow order of the community. Even as a young child she refuses to pretend a conformity that she does not feel. She remembers one of Brigham Young's "progresses" through the settlements when she was a child and the way the whole town turned out to meet him, the little girls all wearing white dresses and carrying flowers to toss in front of his carriage. But young Kate, seeing Brother Brigham "so full of meat, sitting there, and a pretty woman with him, turning her parasol," threw her flowers to the ground and stepped on them. "I couldn't stop him," she remembers, "but I couldn't pretend to love him either. It wasn't honest to throw them and I knew it" (8).

Another of Sorensen's novels, *Many Heavens,* deals not with means of escaping the Mormon community but with the means by which her free spirits can live within it without being dominated by it. The solution, interestingly enough, is found in polygamy. Characteristically, however, Sorensen's sympathetic characters can accept the practice only when the church has given it up. It then becomes a sign of their independence rather than conformity.

Maurine Whipple's *The Giant Joshua* was projected as the first novel in a trilogy exploring "the evolution of the Mormon idea" through three generations (9). Only the first volume was completed, and it is unlikely now that the remainder will ever be written. *The Giant Joshua* has the faults of a first novel: it shows at times too obviously the author's research into pioneer folkways, and its structure deteriorates somewhat in the last third. Nevertheless, it is the most important piece of Mormon regional fiction published thus far.

The setting is what Mormons call "Dixie," the extreme southwestern corner of Utah where Brigham Young sent settlers in the 1860s to grow cotton, the world supply having been disrupted by the Civil War. The settlement of Dixie is synonymous, in Mormon Country, with pioneer hardship and sacrifice. A Mormon folk song concludes with the line, "Heaven help the Dixieite, wherever he may be." And the story is told of the Dixie pioneer who encounters St. Peter at the gates of heaven. "Pass through, Brother," St. Peter says when he learns where the man is from. "You've already had your hell."

The Giant Joshua is told against the background of the ceaseless battle to harness the Virgin River, which comes to symbolize the entire struggle with a remote and inhospitable land. The building of a permanent dam, at the novel's end, symbolizes the community's victory over external obstacles. At the same time the unpalatable, mineralized drinking water of the town symbolizes the threat of internal corruption and conflict that menaces the body of the community even as the water corrupts the innards of those who must drink it.

The novel's protagonist is Clory McIntyre, a third wife in a polygamous family, who gathers in herself several elements of the pioneer myth. She was born into an affluent Philadelphia family. While she was still an infant, her father joined the Mormon church and thereby lost both his wife and his business. He died crossing the plains, and Clory's only brother died in the famine of the first years in the Salt Lake Valley. After her father's death, Clory was reared in the family of Abijah McIntyre, the missionary who had converted her father and himself a man old enough to be her father. Then at 17 she was married to Abijah at Brigham Young's insistence in order to "save" her from a young non-Mormon soldier for whom she felt an attraction.

Clory, then, is almost a compendium of pioneer hardship, but she is not a stereotype. She is a finely realized character of great complexity, and she is like Virginia Sorensen's women, "in the middle," a free spirit who must strain against the discipline of obedience. She is also one of whom obedience makes extraordinary demands. Her situation is most difficult, married to a man she grew up thinking of as an uncle, subjected to the endless hostility of the first wife, Bathsheba, and hopelessly in love with her husband's eldest son, Freeborn (an ironic name in that he is finally destroyed in a futile effort to gain the freedom that should have been his birthright).

Clory has a beautiful and delicate (and unfortunately not very real) daughter whom she loses, together with her two other children, to a plague that strikes the settlement while Abijah is away on a mission to Scotland. To console her, she receives a letter from him informing her that the loss of her children is a punishment for her rebelliousness. By the time she is in her early forties, her beauty is gone and her health broken; Abijah marries a younger wife and moves to another town, leaving Clory and Bathsheba together at last with nothing to quarrel about, leaving Clory also pregnant with the child whose birth kills her.

All of these trials are intensified for Clory because she cannot gain a "testimony," the personal assurance of the rightness of the church that all Mormons are supposed to have. On several occasions she makes up her mind to leave, to find someplace more congenial to her spirit (the title of the novel refers to the Joshua Tree forests of California, a symbol for Clory and Freeborn of a promised land of freedom), but each time something happens to make her remain. With the ambivalence that is almost the hallmark of Mormon regional fiction, she resists the demands of the community and yet finally dies in harness, abandoned by those she would not abandon.

The other characters are less complex than Clory, but some of them are quite interesting nonetheless. Abijah McIntyre is perhaps too broadly drawn to be satisfying, especially to a male reader (one early reviewer, according to Whipple, said, "Lady, lady, I'm not like that" [10]). Nevertheless, he is a perceptive portrait, in some ways, of a man who lacks self-knowledge. The treatment of Erastus Snow, the leader of the colony, is very fine, and so are the brief sketches of Brigham Young: Brigham on his periodic visits checking up on everything, choosing the site for the temple (it turns out to be a swamp into which they have to drive hundreds of tons of rock to establish a firm foundation), instructing on the upbringing of children, even testing a batch of homemade soap and burning his fingers in the process.

Maurine Whipple was "discovered" by John Peale Bishop and Ford Madox Ford at a writers' conference. It was Ford who brought her to the attention of the editors at Houghton Mifflin, who were impressed by the manuscript and excited at the prospect of an eager Mormon audience for the novel. The novel did have a good sale, but not in Mormon Country. Mormon readers (and they are not too much unlike other regional audiences in this) prefer a more idealized treatment of their traditions. The reactions were especially hostile in St. George, Whipple's home town. Her father's comment on the novel was "Well, it's a vulgar book" (11). These reactions by the people she knew best had much to do, I believe, with the withering of Whipple's talent.

Virginia Sorensen also has gained only a slight acceptance by the regional audience. Her chief commercial success is as a writer of children's books. Yet such is the hold of the region that Maurine Whipple lives on in St. George among her red rocks and indifferent townspeople. Virginia Sorensen lives in Tangier, Morocco, with her husband Alec Waugh, but she too claims that she intends someday to return to Utah, "having found no place in the world more beautiful or satisfying" (12). And that, I suppose, is the voice of the regionalist.

NOTES

1. Bernard DeVoto, "Vacation," *Harper's* 177 (Oct. 1938): 560.
2. Whipple published only one novel, *The Giant Joshua* (Boston: Houghton Mifflin, 1942). Sorensen's Mormon fiction includes *A Little Lower than the Angels*

(New York: Knopf, 1942); *On This Star* (New York: Reynal & Hitchcock, 1946); *The Evening and the Morning* (New York: Harcourt, 1949); *Many Heavens* (New York: Harcourt, 1954); *Kingdom Come* (New York: Harcourt, 1960); and *Where Nothing Is Long Ago: Memories of a Mormon Childhood* (New York: Harcourt, 1963).

Other notable Mormon regional novels include Jean Woodman, *Glory Spent* (New York: Carrick & Evans, 1940); Paul Bailey, *For This Is My Glory* (Los Angeles: Lymanhouse, 1940); Lorene Pearson, *The Harvest Waits* (Indianapolis: Bobbs Merrill, 1941); Elinor Pryor, *And Never Yield* (New York: Macmillan, 1942); Richard P. Scowcroft, *Children of the Covenant* (Boston: Houghton Mifflin, 1945); Blanche Cannon, *Nothing Ever Happens Sunday Morning* (New York: G. P. Putnam's Sons, 1948); Ardyth Kennelly, *The Peaceable Kingdom* (Boston: Houghton Mifflin, 1949); and Samuel W. Taylor, *Family Kingdom* (New York: McGraw-Hill, 1951).

3. Wallace Stegner, *The Sound of Mountain Water: The Changing American West* (Garden City, NY: Doubleday, 1969), p. 178.
4. "Maurine Whipple's Story of *The Giant Joshua*," as told to Maryruth Bracy and Linda Lambert, *Dialogue: A Journal of Mormon Thought* 6 (Winter 1971): 56–57.
5. Virginia Sorensen, "Is It True?—The Novelist and His Materials," *Western Humanities Review* 7 (1953): 284. Further references to this article will be indicated by page number in the text.
6. Sorensen, *Where Nothing Is Long Ago,* 5. Other references to this novel will be indicated by page number in the text.
7. Sorensen, "Is It True?" 285.

8. Sorensen, *The Evening and the Morning,* 21.
9. "Maurine Whipple's Story of *The Giant Joshua,*" 56.
10. Ibid., 60.
11. Ibid., 58
12. *Contemporary Authors,* 1st rev., vols. 13–16, ed. Clare D. Kinsman (Detroit: Gale Research Co., 1975), 755.

VI

Rediscovery

Chapter 9

Living, Loving, Learning
Edith Gleckler's THE REBIRTH OF JACOB WINNINGSTADT

By Bernard J. Koloski

Author's Note: In May 1976 I spoke to the Friends of the Library at Mansfield State College in north-central Pennsylvania about Kate Chopin and other turn-of-the-century novelists. Among the women who stopped afterward to chat was a retired English teacher with fluffy snow-white hair and an impish grin who said, "My mother wrote a novel just a few years after Kate Chopin wrote hers." No, it had not been published, she told me, and yes, she would let me examine it.

Throughout the next week I spent several hours a day at Marion Gleckler's little house a block from our campus, carefully reading a fragile-looking manuscript titled *The Rebirth of Jacob Winningstadt*. I tried at first to repress my growing excitement but quickly gave in to it as I realized that the novel was more than historically accurate, that it had captured the spirit of both the land and the people of north-central Pennsylvania.

Since then I've learned a good deal about Edith Gleckler and her times, and I've found a deep satisfaction in coming to know *The Rebirth of Jacob Winningstadt*. My colleague Celeste Sexauer and I have now completed preparing the novel for publication. We hope it will soon become available to readers.

"Don't attempt to write," Edith Gleckler told her daughter Marion. "It's too heart-breaking when it's not accepted, and you never know what skill you have until it's too late to do much about it. Just let it go." She spoke from experience. She had labored for years on the 65,000 words of *The Rebirth of Jacob Winningstadt* (1), writing during the hours she could set aside from her duties as wife, mother, teacher, school board member, and mistress of a 15-room farmhouse near Liberty, Pennsylvania.

For a frustrating half-decade between 1911 and 1916 she searched for a publisher, receiving only rejections from legitimate houses and solicitations from not especially competent vanity presses. Nothing in her background had prepared her to deal with publishers in Boston, St. Paul, Baltimore, or Springfield, Ohio (2). Although she was, like one of the characters in her novel, a "woman of more culture and refinement than most of the women in the neighborhood," she had spent her entire life among the farms and schools of north-central Pennsylvania. Born in 1868 in Lawrenceville, on the New York border, she grew up there and later studied at the nearby normal school in Mansfield. When she began her teaching career outside the little community of Liberty, she was within 50 miles of her birthplace.

The publishers' rejections eventually were disheartening. Edith Gleckler continued to write essays for local newspapers and remained active in her public life as a member of the Liberty school board, working tirelessly to upgrade the rural education system in the area. When her farm duties became too strenuous for her, she moved in 1919 with her husband and daughter to Mansfield, relishing the educational and cultural activities there. She took her novel with her, making some careful revisions and having a typed copy prepared. But she did not resubmit it for publication, and at her death in 1927 it was put aside with her other papers in a bedroom of her home.

Fifty years later *The Rebirth of Jacob Winningstadt* is still not available to readers, but it is worth making available and worth thinking about. While it is not a polished book—Edith Gleckler knew that she would have learned a great deal from a good editor—it is a many-faceted work of fiction: a regional novel, a local color novel, an expression of its author's natural optimism and natural enjoyment of people, as well as an educational reform document, a complaint about the rapid physical deterioration of farm women, a plea for emotional and spiritual regeneration, and most important, a blueprint for a culture's continued survival.

At the center of the book is an affirmation of a way of life that the author realizes is in desperate need of radical transformation. Edith Gleckler sets out to make her work a loving picture of life on the farms of Liberty Valley around 1900. She would like, she says in her foreword, "to preserve for future generations some of the richly picturesque scenes of this unique Valley, and to carry down to them the many neighborly, homely, kindly customs of these dear, gentle, thrifty people."

Like the local color writers of her time, she captures the

deep satisfaction of an existence she understands intimately: Four farm wives sit on wood-bottomed chairs in a summer kitchen, quartering Golden Sweet apples, placing them in a large tub, animatedly sharing their concerns about their children; a couple rides slowly in a buggy as dawn breaks through a curtain of fog hanging over a frost-enveloped landscape of shrubs and hemlocks, ferns and moss-covered rocks; a young boy fastens a piece of salt pork to a stick so he can stir the boiling maple syrup in a large evaporator, watching with delight as the steam condenses into drops on the eaves of the slate roof above him; eighteen men, dusty from the oats they have been threshing, banter with one another across a table set with gigantic dishes of chicken, ham, mashed potatoes, pickled eggs, white bread, mince pie, and coffee. *The Rebirth of Jacob Winningstadt* validates through local experience traditional national values, and for Edith Gleckler the greatest of values are those she sees growing out of the rural environment itself—family, friendship, love of the land, and individual growth made possible through the support and the warm encouragement of the group.

Yet many of those values, she recognizes, are wanting in her time. Liberty Valley continued at the turn of the century to be caught up in an economic decline that threatened both the beauty of the land and the way of life that had evolved on it. The forests in the area had been stripped of much of their best timber, especially their best hemlock, leaving behind barren mountaintops. Extensive soft-coal mining had created ugly open areas of waste top land. The mountainous terrain and a soil laden with glacial rock made many of the newer farming methods difficult and expensive.

The habits of frugality and diligence, of industry and thrift that had created and nourished the culture of Liberty Valley in the early nineteenth century were by themselves inadequate for a society's survival 100 years later. People had been abandoning their farms and settling in urban areas. And many of those who stayed behind had, like the title character of the novel, allowed themselves to become "narrow-minded" and "egotistical," clinging out of fear to the old values. "This skimming process," one of the women in the novel complains, "of taking away the best brain and leaving the ignorant and undeveloped on the farms has been going on for generations here." "We are," one of the men insists, "not being driven westward, but inward toward the centers of civilization. It will soon be take to the city or practically live here alone."

So affirmation for Edith Gleckler necessarily involves change, growth, challenge, transformation. *The Rebirth of Jacob Winningstadt* fully captures Edith Gleckler's joyous response to life, but its primary emphasis comes to settle on her rich personal vision of how the rural schools could restore to the people of Liberty Valley the source of their strength.

The plot of the novel is an acting out of such a vision, "a story," the author notes, "of a man who looked backward, of a man who looked forward, and of a girl with wisdom who saw between." Jacob Winningstadt can understand only the necessity of preserving the old traditions. He farms as his father and grandfather did. Although his crops and his timberlands are profitable, he denies to himself, his wife, his sons, and his daughter Jennie the material comforts their labor has earned for them. His other four children have already abandoned the farm, all without an inheritance, and Fred, his oldest son, is rapidly approaching a physical collapse from overwork in a nearby city. As president of the Liberty school board, Jacob concentrates on keeping taxes low by hiring mostly untrained teachers, refusing to consider the need for a high school, and trying to avoid state regulations that set minimum standards for the education of children.

Walter Darmhurst, Jacob's neighbor and fellow school board member, realizes that Jacob's attitude toward farming and education reflects the beliefs of most Liberty Valley inhabitants. He has, however, made his own farm a model of both productivity and comfort, and since he is, like Jacob's daughter Jennie, a graduate of the local normal school, he understands the power of education as a tool for social change. He recognizes that the economic recovery of the area requires modern farming techniques adapted to the mountainous terrain and rocky soil and that good rural schools are the best media through which people can be brought to an understanding of such techniques and therefore to a new sense of hope and confidence about themselves and their way of life. For Edith Gleckler it is a crucial point:

> *There is beauty enough in every farm locality to satisfy the longings of any artistic soul. There is enough to study and to learn about. There is enough of God's handiwork to inspire men and women to the highest culture. It is the unobstructed field of the dreamer or the worker, the poet or the philosopher. But its beauties and its wonders must be pointed out to these common people before they will utilize their wealth to enhance their lives and make them full and complete. This is the work of the rural school.*

Walter and Jacob struggle throughout most of the novel for control of the school system, yet when the necessary change in Jacob occurs, its motive force comes not from economics or education but from the hero's deepened personal insight, from his emotional and spiritual growth. His daughter Jennie, who sees between the backward-looking Jacob and the forward-looking Walter Darmhurst, her husband-to-be, has always understood her father's capacity to act as "a power for good" in the area, and she loves the man "as none of his other children" do because she has "gotten under the rough exterior to his well meaning heart."

Jennie perceives the damage done to her area in general and to her family in particular in primarily human terms. She knows that her older brothers and sisters abandoned the farm because they could endure neither the relentless work nor their father's rigid insensitivity to their needs or desires, and she knows that it is merely a matter of months before her remaining two brothers are likely to leave. She realizes that with her brothers gone, her parents will need to give up their farm as so many of their neighbors have done, because hired help is nearly impossible to come by in the area. And she understands clearly what Edith Gleckler makes into a persistent theme throughout the novel: the devastating effect of continuous farmwork on the health of her mother, on the health of nearly all of the wives and daughters of land owners.

Although the author speaks at one point in the book about "motherhood" as women's "God-intended mission upon this earth"—and she no doubt accepts the idea—her voice becomes harsh and even bitter as she describes Jacob Winningstadt's treating his wife "with less consideration than he did his horses":

> *When I say with less consideration, I mean this: when his horses lost their appetite or flesh and seemed to lack ambition, he got condition powders and fed them, or changed their diet. But when any or all of these symptoms appeared in his wife he did not notice it. Secondly, when his horses worked a reasonable day with a*

> *good noon hour, he refused to let them be driven nights, even when it would have given his family much pleasure. But the day was never so long,* without *the noon hour, that his wife could not sit up all night with a sick child—their own or a neighbor's—and work the next day. Thirdly, while his horses pranced resplendent in silver-plated harnesses, his wife wore a bonnet or coat as long as the things held together. She turned, colored, and made over her dresses, and of course looked shabby and old fashioned.*

Like so many of the women in the novel, Jennie's mother has experienced marriage to a farmer as "years of toil and privation, years of self-denial and servitude." At age 50 "she had the appearance of a woman who had run her allotted time. She might be able to stand the strain of work ten years longer, but they would likely be followed by years of pain and suffering."

Jennie has tried to lead her father to understand that his hard work, dedication, and prudence are not in themselves adequate expressions of love for his wife and children, just as his frugality with his neighbors' tax money does not in itself help the schools offer to the young people in the Valley the support and guidance that would encourage them to remain on the farms. Jacob cannot be moved through economic or educational arguments. His ties to the past, his need to maintain the old traditions, to pass on to the next generation the values that were passed on to him, constitute a way of thought too deeply ingrained to be affected by rational discussion.

It is, Edith Gleckler makes clear, ultimately the pull of the old values themselves that brings about Jacob Winningstadt's rebirth. The hero responds immediately and instinctively to his oldest son's near-fatal illness, slowly nursing him back to health; and out of that response there grows for him a transformed vision of how family closeness and community support could become a reality again within the economic and educational structure dreamed of by Walter and Jennie.

When Jacob is able to recognize that his treatment of his son had been potentially destructive, then he can understand that he has treated his wife and his other children in a similar way. And he can see also that, largely through his leadership as president of the school board, he and his neighbors in Liberty Valley have withheld financial and emotional support from their sons and daughters. His emotional "awakening" at a moment of personal crisis leads him to a deeper perception of his responsibility not only as a father but as a husband and a member of the community as well, and he sets out to put personal, economic, and educational reforms into action. For Edith Gleckler there is no difficulty in grasping Plato's insistence that to know the Good is to perform the Good.

That is no doubt why the author discarded the original title of her novel, *A Prince of the Soil,* with its focus on Walter Darmhurst, the visionary who has already made his farm prosperous and who already knows how to use the rural schools to kindle enthusiasm for modern farming among the young people in the area. It is, Edith Gleckler realizes, not the Walters but the Jacobs of Liberty Valley who must experience an awakening if the society she loves is to survive much longer. It is the Jacobs who must grow toward an insight about the "wonderful possibilities" in themselves and in the rural Pennsylvania way of life.

And that is also why *The Rebirth of Jacob Winningstadt* has for its author a value that far transcends its regional emphasis, its local color flavor, its concern for the condition of farm women. Edith Gleckler is writing not only *about* the people of Liberty Valley but *for* those people as well. Her primary purpose clearly approaches what Lionel Trilling argues must be the goal of any novel, "the restoration and reconstitution of the will." Edith Gleckler would smile sadly to learn that her book is being discussed a half-century after its completion. Much in her culture that she sought to affirm and transform has long ago passed from existence.

NOTES

1. The manuscript of *The Rebirth of Jacob Winningstadt* and of several essays, poems, articles, and other works written by Edith Gleckler have been made available to me through an arrangement with Marion Gleckler, her trustees, and the Mansfield State College Foundation.
2. *Farm and Fireside* magazine in Springfield, Ohio, turned down the manuscript in 1911. The Roxburgh Company in Boston, publishers of "high class fiction," offered in 1912 to print 1,500 copies of the novel in return for $400, and encouraged the author to seriously consider such an offer because, while the book was, Roxburgh felt, "crude in literary finish, still it, and through its crudeness here and there, lacks that see-same literary effectation so common, and this identical originality may be its strong point in universal commend [*sic*]." A. M. Burchall of the McLean Company of 7 Clay Street in Baltimore agreed in 1916 to publish the novel for $500 or without cost if the author would "supervise" the sale of 800 copies of a McLean book called *Garden of Faith*. And Ada Melville Shaw, associate editor of *The Farmer's Wife* magazine in St. Paul, rejected what Edith Gleckler had sent her, but sympathized with the problems caused by what she called the "grafters" and "sharks" in the publishing industry. "There is a great deal of this work done, my dear Miss Gleckler," she wrote, "and women writers especially are the victims sought after because of their inexperience."

VII

New Definitions

Chapter 10

Regions of the Mind and Margaret Gibson Gilboord's THE BUTTERFLY WARD

By Arnold E. Davidson

Regionalism as commonly discussed refers to writings set in locations other than the acknowledged centers of "civilization." No one has to assert the claims of the actual loci of power or argue that such sites demand our attention. They have it already, preponderantly so. In fact, the celebration of the rural land and the small community that is so much a part of the tradition of regional writing is partly a reaction against the general social denigration of just such places. Willa Cather extols the Nebraska prairies at least in part to counter the more common myth of a featureless, empty land inhabited mostly by gophers and a few surly, backward farmers. Sarah Orne Jewett praises a rugged New England—which does not extend into Boston. The regional writer, to portray place, must also re-create the place in a new image designed to supersede the generally demeaning stereotype.

In the best regional tradition Margaret Gibson Gilboord's *The Butterfly Ward* describes and redefines a particular world that is often misperceived. The locus in her fiction, however, is not Toronto, where the stories physically take place. Toronto is hardly a "region" for a Canadian, for it is the cultural center of the nation. Gilboord looks, instead, at a psychic region, a region as alien to the bustling crowds of Toronto as it would be to the inhabitants of Saskatoon, Saskatchewan. This author's region is the human mind and, more specifically, the realm of the schizophrenic whose own unreality provides a kind of landscape in which "normal" human beings can be as trees or mountains or other topographical features—elements that are simply *other*. Gilboord explores this world with sensitivity and compassion. In doing so, she also re-creates a sense of the place to counter the conventional distortions perpetrated by those who have written of the region but who have never journeyed there.

It should here be noted that Gilboord has, indeed, traveled through the world she writes of. She has acknowledged that she has been diagnosed as a paranoid schizophrenic and has spoken openly about her own condition, about how periods of lucidity and "normality" are inexplicably and uncontrollably interrupted by periods of paranoia. She has described how a generally accepted view of reality suddenly will be replaced by a private and more pressing "reality" that is generally deemed insane. Consequently, she can feel that she is, like any other minority writer, largely defined by her condition. So in this sense she is an outsider in a world elsewhere, a regionalist of the mind.

This Canadian woman "regionalist" has written a book of short stories that has not yet received the recognition that it deserves, even though one of these stories, "Making It," was the basis for the recent Cannes Film Festival Award–wining movie, OUTRAGEOUS. But that story itself can provide an appropriate starting point for assessing the achievement of Margaret Gibson Gilboord, for it effectively illustrates both the substance and the scope of the other tales that, with it, comprise *The Butterfly Ward*. "Making It" is an account of how two outcasts—a female schizophrenic and a male homosexual female impersonator—attempt to make it in the "straight" world. Based on the author's long-lasting friendship with Craig Russell (a female impersonator), the story is loosely autobiographical.

Like the other stories in the volume, this one criticizes the straight world from a perspective outside that world, even while it shows society's rejects trying to survive in a society in which they have no place. In other words, the region is a microcosm reflecting the macrocosm. *But* the region itself, the small world within the larger, is the focus of the fiction and in many ways is more important than the larger world that most of us already know. "Making It," like most of the other stories in *The Butterfly Ward*, is also partly about how the macrocosm defines and even "creates" the microcosm in its own image. In this respect, the book particularly illustrates the gender-orientation of mental illness, the way insanity is both diagnosed and "cured" according to traditional expectations regarding what constitutes acceptable female and male behavior (1).

The story itself is told in a series of letters between Liza and Robin. They had lived together, platonically, until he left for California, where he hoped to become famous by impersonating such famous women as Bette Davis, Tallulah Bankhead, Peggy Lee, Mae West, and others whom Liza, even though female, could not begin to imitate. Obviously transvestism does not preclude a masculine concern with achieving success. As Robin writes Liza: "I don't want to die an old fag alone, without lovers, without a certain amount of respect, I want to say—I made it once, me. I made it. Don't you want to make it, Liza? I am tired of being always less than good in the world's eyes" (2).

Robin wants to succeed through his career. Liza also desperately wants to "make it," but in the way culturally expected of women. She wants to be a mother. To achieve that objective, she sleeps with a cabdriver who takes her to her psychiatrist's office. That encounter appropriately conjoins both the fate she is trying to avoid with her pregnancy (mental illness) and the insignificance of the man involved: "The father of this baby is nothing, he has less substance than the frost on the windowpane" (page 114). Both anonymous and irrelevant, the man is merely a means to an end. But the end—motherhood—is crucial if Liza is to achieve the normality she identifies as sanity.

In answer to Robin's question about making it, Liza writes explaining her concept of the "Great Divider" and the way he can be defeated:

> *The Great Divider is what made you and me. He is bone splitting. He is what kept us away and apart from other people. You could not divide the he-she in your being and I—I could not stop the bone splitting, dividing into nightmares and hallucinations and breathing floors. Somewhere in the void you and I met, walking and wounded and collapsed into each other's arms, but we cannot give in to him now, to his pile of bones, split asunder, he would be the winner if we gave in, right now we hang on by the edge of our teeth.* The baby will have me a few steps removed from the Great Divider and so will your career. . . . *Don't you see, the Great Divider is Defeat, the Defeat we were born with and now we have a chance to out-distance him and we must. (pages 115–116; emphasis added)*

In other words, the Great Divider is not just fate, time, entropy. "He" is also the nether regions of their beings,

Robin's homosexuality and Liza's schizophrenia. Success for him and motherhood for her, will erase the boundaries that separate these two rejects from the "real" world. A famous homosexual is still famous, rewarded by society. And can a mother be insane?

In its own way, "Making It" is a love story, but it is a love story with a difference. Whereas conventional love stories give us further fuzzy images of the myths we would believe in, this one more clearly reflects the psychic and social world we inhabit and shows how romantic myths function in that world. Like many of the female protagonists in Gilboord's stories, Liza has a fantasy about love, marriage, motherhood—all must conduce to happiness ever after. She represses the sordid details of the conception and fantasizes that Robin—Bette, Peggy, Tallulah, Mae, as she addresses him in various letters—is the real father of the child she will bear. By the end of the story, Robin too has begun to participate in the fantasy. For both of them, it is a fantasy of normality: he will be a father; she will be a mother; they will have a child. Society will approve. As a simple nuclear "family" they can defeat the Great Divider. Robin canvasses Los Angeles looking for an apartment with "a nice, bright room for a nursery and a good kitchen. You used to make the most terrific chili" (page 117). On one of his searches he meets "the most beautiful man . . . and he offered to buy me a drink but I said no—there is no time for that now" (page 117). A father-fantasy briefly dispels Robin's "normal" (for him) sexual desires. He is caught up in being the provider, the head of household. He buys things for the baby—a stuffed bear, a Winnie-the-Pooh record. When a stripper mentions that they also will need a layette, he writes Liza asking her what a layette is.

Liza's answer, her last letter, is conclusive tribute to the power of the Great Divider: "A layette is clothing for the baby like a white gown and booties. Vanessa was born dead" (page 118). Robin's response to this shocking announcement is only the beginning of a letter, "Dear Liza." The blank page better expresses his inconsolable grief, and hers. That empty page marks the death of the child and the dashed hopes of two people thrust back into the non-identities they pretend to, but never really could, escape.

The language of Liza's last letter also implies her abrupt return to her own mental world, that other region beyond the socially acceptable one. The "white gown and booties" are ominous, a hospital gown, a death shroud. The death of Vanessa also suggests that hope had rested on this unborn child who was named and given an identity and a function before she was born, dead. But more is at issue than just the insubstantiality of the protagonists' dreams. The ambitions of both Robin and Liza, the demand for normality and social acceptance, prompt us to question normal values. Marriage should solve all problems? A child should solve any marital problems? We, the *sane* readers, know that a child and the semblance of a monogamous marriage—bright nursery, well-equipped kitchen—cannot resolve the difficulties in these characters' lives. But, Gilboord implies, in the sane world these are exactly the tokens of happiness that we do accept as the real thing.

In other ways, too, Gilboord shows that the sane world is not so far removed from the insane world as the reader might hope. In one scene, a "straight" man propositions Robin and then is disappointed to encounter only Robin, not Tallulah or Marilyn back from the dead. Liza must twice a week play the stereotypical expectant mother in order to appease the public health nurse who checks on her and who is responsible for her welfare money. Liza must "function," which means she must smile (but not too widely or too often). She must serve acceptable coffee. She must keep her apartment and herself clean and neat. She must be readying the nursery. In short, she must pretend to be "normal." Much like Robin who wants to be such a good female impersonator that people *will* think he's Marilyn or Mae, Liza wants to be the Ivory Soap mother. Beyond that naïve dream is the author's implicit question: If success and normality are as restrictive as this, is making it really worth it? Is the sane world truly sane?

Gilboord goes even further in questioning "conventional" behavior. In Robin's letter about finding an apartment, we see him playing the standard masculine role. He describes the nursery for the child, the kitchen for the mother. Both will keep him from the beautiful men with whom he would prefer to associate. He realizes that living with Liza will not satisfy his sexual self, but at least he will enjoy her chili. A woman, for this impersonator of famous women, is one who mothers, cooks, nurtures. His stereotype means that her life should become one-dimensional, and because of his sexual preferences, life with her will limit his life, too. We watch two misfits play at normality in a fantasy effort to appease both society and their own awareness that they are society's rejects. Again Gilboord implicitly criticizes a society that forces people into such unsatisfying stereotypical roles. As "father" and "mother," Robin and Liza would become citizens of the larger world. But once more one wonders whether the admission is worth the price.

Most of the stories in *The Butterfly Ward* turn on similar issues, defining the regions of the haunted mind (almost always a female mind) both in its own right and in relationship to the reality of the "sane" world. But if these stories substantially question society's definition of *normative* female behavior, "Considering Her Condition" asks how insane a man can be without being deemed abnormal. In that bleak but brilliant story, Stephen Davis, "a part-time writer and full-time unit manager of a large and rather prestigious television station" (page 51), hides himself behind his camera. His disturbed vision, transformed into art, becomes laudable. So too he translates in other ways. His wife, whose own emotional disturbances have been rigorously analyzed and officially diagnosed, becomes his primary "subject," in all the ways suggested by that term: he rules over her, he experiments with her, he writes about her in his ever-present journal. He encourages her insecurities, her psychoses—both make good copy.

Their unhealthy relationship is another mirror of conventional marriage and conventional gender-designations within marriage. She exists for her husband and for motherhood. Even her suicide, after the birth of his son, makes little difference. He can still write about her. In fact, his final statements regarding his deceased wife indicate that he is hardly disturbed by her death at all: "She seemed more tangible now in death than she ever had in life. And, I never wanted to have children with anyone but her, as strange as that may sound, considering her condition" (page 78). But with this last phrase Gilboord especially requires us to consider *his* condition.

Although the disturbed characters in Gilboord's fiction are members of a minority group, and definitely oppressed, most of them still emerge as sympathetic characters who are often surprisingly strong. Liza and Robin are outcasts who also see themselves as outcasts. They do not realize that their heterosexual but asexual friendship—their deep love, trust, and caring for one another—is a rarity in any world, even (maybe especially) in the so-called normal world. Jenny, the main character and narrator of "Ada," tries to block out the more disturbing aspects of her asylum life. But she feels compassion for her friend Ada and contempt for those in the medical establishment who have reduced Ada almost to a human vegetable. In the title story, "The Butterfly Ward," Kira escapes the horrors of a brutal medical procedure partly by imagining herself as a butterfly. Her fantasies are a kind of poetry and a further illustration of how human this world, ostensibly beyond normal humanity, can be.

As Laurence Ricou has observed in a recent review, Gilboord portrays both the "agony and the lyrical clarity of people going mad" (3). Yet she does not glorify insanity or sentimentalize it. She allows the reader entry into a world seldom seen from the inside:

> *Sometimes it can be beautiful inside this space. Most people who can ride on buses and streetcars and eat doughnuts for breakfast if and when they want and don't have to dial 0 on their phones to make a call would think that statement crazy. Maybe it is a bit crazy. (page 119)*

Gilboord's ambiguous use of "crazy" in that quotation is typical. She defuses the supposedly denigrating even while she employs it. Essentially, that is what all of her stories do. They portray characters who are "a bit crazy." But they also portray a world that is "a bit crazy." Like the best regional writers, Gilboord forces readers to reevaluate preconceived notions and to reincorporate into their world view what had previously been dismissed. She shows that there are no clear maps conveniently demarcating the boundaries between sanity and insanity. When we finish *The Butterfly Ward,* it is difficult to know whether or not we still remain outside the borders of the place described or whether we have crossed over into the other territory—as trespassers or as citizens.

NOTES

1. For a much more substantial and technical consideration of many of the points briefly discussed in this article, see Phyllis Chesler, *Women and Madness* (Gar-

den City, NY: Doubleday, 1972), especially chaps. 1, 2, and 10.
2. Margaret Gibson Gilboord, *The Butterfly Ward* (Toronto: Oberon Press, 1976), 111; all page references to this edition.
3. Laurence Ricou, "Story and Teller," *Canadian Literature*, No. 76 (1978): 118.

Chapter 11

Anti-American Regionalism in the Fiction of Doris Lessing

By Katherine Fishburn

Of all of Doris Lessing's themes, perhaps the most puzzling is her avid anti-Americanism, the presence of which inevitably raises the question: why does such a strong opponent of labeling stoop to what resembles nothing more than chauvinistic name-calling? I think the answer to this lies in Lessing's philosophy, which is, basically, a belief that the world is a single organism, capable of infinite progress but continually subject to attack from within.

Never a nationalist herself, Lessing is known nevertheless for expressing her philosophy in political terms. To illustrate her ideas, however, she often uses the customs not of her own country, as we might expect, but those of another—the United States. Time and again in her fiction, through a sort of obverse (or perverse) regionalism, she unmercifully exposes the weaknesses of America, in gestures less calculated to be accurate representation than significant hyperbole.

This is not to say that England does not appear in her

work, because London, next to the human mind, is probably her single most important landscape (1). But even London, with all its streets and shops, does not inform her writing with the impact of a region. In other words, London is Lessing's background, but it is not her object of focus. It is instead America, with its power and influence, that draws her attention. It does so because her province is the psyche, and in her eyes, the greatest threat to the psyche at this time can be symbolized most precisely by the United States of America.

Lessing, of course, is not alone in her strident attacks on Americans. She is keeping fast company with some of the best British satirists of our day: Kingsley Amis, John Wain, John Bowen, and Keith Waterhouse. But if the effect of their satire is humor, the final effect of Lessing's is disquietude. To be sure, we laugh along with Lessing and her Americans as she laughs at them and they laugh at themselves, but it is an uneasy laughter. It could very well be uneasy, because we don't like the way she has characterized us, but I think the situation is more complex than this. I think that Lessing sees the dangerous consequences of living in the modern world as being most clearly exemplified by the behavior of Americans. Her purpose in satirizing us, therefore, is to warn everyone, of all nations, against the perils of living in a self-indulgent, aggressive, highly industrialized society, especially one as powerful as the United States. And our uncomfortable response is less aggrieved nationalism than fear in an age of uncertainty.

Lessing's urgent drive to satirize us, however, has not always been a feature of her fiction. In her earliest work there is no trace of either America or its citizens. This absence can be explained by the fact that Lessing was writing about her home in Southern Rhodesia, an essentially insular agrarian society that in 1940 had not yet begun to feel the full effects of what James Gindin calls "creeping

Americanism" (2). And what influence there was in the African cities, Lessing admits she was blind to. "I had not seen the society as American," she writes in her journal, *Going Home*, "because I [had] been hypnotized by the word *British*" (3). America, therefore, plays no role in Lessing's African stories and novels. Once she moved to England in 1949, however, her perception of life changed markedly, a change that is reflected in her fiction.

Immigrating to the land all British colonials dream of and consider their true home no matter where they have been born and raised, Lessing was deeply affected by the appearance of postwar London. Although she does not specifically mention the legacy from the Americans stationed there (that Keith Waterhouse satirizes in his novel *Billy Liar*), it is from this point on that her writing acknowledges the American presence in the world.

When she returned in 1956 to southern Africa, for example, she was able, as she records in *Going Home*, to see how Americanized Salisbury was. Driving through town, seeing its "pretty houses with their patios" and its "mass of reckless, undisciplined cars," she realizes "suddenly and for the first time that this was an American small town; it is the town we have all seen in a hundred films about Mom and Pop and their family problems" (page 50). As she travels through the countryside, she is struck more than once by the ubiquity of that most successful American emissary of goodwill—the Coke bottle. "Above all," she writes, "Coca-Cola has moved in. The Coca-Cola sign is on every second building, from the high new blocks of offices and flats to the scruffy little store in the Native Reserve" (page 52). Other identifying features of American life that Lessing sees here are the myths of the "frontiersman and the lone-wolf; the brave white woman home-making in lonely and primitive conditions; the child who gets himself an education and so a status beyond his parents" (page

51)—not to mention the blue-jean-sweatshirt-and-slang culture that has infiltrated southern Africa. Although her observations about the United States in *Going Home* generally are not related directly to politics, by simple repetition, they do assume a political significance. It is clear from what she says in *Going Home* that by the time she returned to England, Doris Lessing was no longer able to ignore America. This is manifested in the anti-American regionalism that emerged shortly thereafter in her fiction.

The first of her novels to reflect this anti-Americanism was *The Golden Notebook* (1962). Just how many Americans are in it is difficult to determine because of the novel's complex, overlapping structure and the fact that many people appear in different notebooks with different names. Suffice it to say that all of the Americans in this novel are troubled by basically the same problems: they are slick, tough, and lonely people. For example, the first time the American called Nelson (no last name) appears, he is described quite satirically as being in the process of writing the American masterpiece and as being separated from his neurotic wife. The satiric quality of this information is evident in the tone of the passage in which the protagonist, Anna Wulf (who is also known as Ella), describes him to her friend Molly Jacobs. According to Anna, who condenses his life with almost brutal simplicity, Nelson "left his wife. Because she was neurotic. Got himself a girl. Very nice one. Decided she was neurotic. Went back to his wife. Decided she was neurotic. Left her. Has got himself another girl who so far hasn't become neurotic" (4). When Molly asks Anna about the other Americans living in London, Anna replies, "In one way and another, ditto, ditto, ditto" (page 51). By using these clipped sentences that, for the most part, have no subjects, Lessing reinforces her view that all Americans are virtually interchangeable, rather pitiful robots who wander randomly through life in jerky little predictable patterns.

Because Nelson is dissatisfied with his wife, he ultimately seeks a "real relationship" with Anna. In bed with her, he fluctuates between entertaining her with what she calls his "American self-punishing humor" (page 483) and hysterically abusing all women, including her. Two weeks later, in a moment of reconciliation between them, Anna suddenly sees that "glass wall certain kinds of Americans live behind," that barrier that says "don't touch me, for God's sake don't touch me, don't touch me because I'm afraid of feeling" (page 485). This attitude is typical of all the Americans in Lessing's fiction, as they insulate themselves against all possible hurt by maintaining a safe distance between themselves and other people, even—and sometimes especially—their spouses and lovers (5).

To reinforce her view of Americans as hopelessly neurotic, Lessing follows this scene of genuine communication between Anna and Nelson with a brilliant parody of an American cocktail party. Through this party, given by Nelson and his wife at their "large rented flat, full of tasteless, anonymous furniture" (page 486), Lessing satirizes the emotional sterility that she perceives in Americans. Written as dialogue in a play, the scene inevitably calls for comparison with Edward Albee's *Who's Afraid of Virginia Woolf?*, as Nelson and his wife publicly flay each other with vicious barbs thinly disguised as good-humored ribbing. Like Albee's George, Nelson is only minimally successful in his work, and like Albee's Martha, his wife is too eager to promote his meager talents. So his wife attacks and he counterattacks, while the hysteria mounts and the laughter increases—the laughter that lies between them and their fear. Even the dancing that in the end saves the party from its potentially explosive conclusion is seen negatively by Anna as a parody of good-humored sexy dancing.

In addition to Nelson, Anna-Ella takes other American men as lovers, none of whom is able truly to please her. Cy Maitland, for example, is a man who is traveling through life on the American plan. That is, he is using his brains to get ahead. No slouch, he has also discovered a way to use other people's brains: he makes his living by performing leucotomies (lobotomies). To his friends, his life seems to be perfect. But Cy, who sees the fatal division between illusion and reality, tells Ella with self-mocking irony that he married the prettiest girl in town, who gave him five beautiful children, and now he has plans to become a United States Senator. The hitch in his so-called perfect life, of course, is that his pretty spouse doesn't like sex.

Without much effort Ella is able to discover why: a brilliant brain surgeon, Cy Maitland is a sexual illiterate, with a bedside manner that would cool any lady's passions. In what is a truly comic, if also sad scene, Lessing delivers the crowning blow to the myth of American maleness as the future senator from Wyoming takes less than ten seconds to reach sexual climax, much to Ella's understandable dismay. Although Cy is definitely a hick (ordering Coke in the restaurant while Ella orders wine, and forcing the rather timid Ella to proposition him), he is a good-natured hick, and Ella likes him in spite of his gaucherie. Tempted briefly to enlighten him about his sexual incompetence, she instead allows him to return to Wyoming full of wonder that such liberated, trouble-free women as Ella exist (pages 319–30).

Although one might predict, after this scene, that Lessing would be more tolerant of American women than she is of their men (out of sympathy if nothing else), this is not the case. For example, Anna describes Nelson's wife as attractive but shrill, with a superficial self-assurance Anna (and presumably Lessing) finds common to all American women. These women, according to Anna, "have a nervous, frightened look to their shoulders. They are frightened. They look as if they were out in a space somewhere by themselves, pretending that they are not alone" (page 487). In their isolation and desperate need to cover it up, they frighten Anna. Nelson's wife in particular is locked permanently in a controlled hysteria, from which she compulsively hounds her husband, fearful above all that she will lose him and thus her security and her sense of self-worth.

Her behavior resembles that of Edwina Wright, a talent scout for an American TV-film series, who visits London to interview Anna about adapting her South African best-selling novel, *Frontiers of War,* for American television. Mrs. Wright is 45 or 50, "with iron-grey hair, curled and shining; gleaming blue-grey lids; shining pink lips; shining pale-pink nails. A suit of soft blue, very expensive. An expensive woman" (page 290). Over dinner, she is solicitous and tactful, making Anna feel as if she is being taken out by a man. And yet, accomplished as Mrs. Wright is at playing this role of host, it is one with which she is not comfortable, as she reveals by drinking four martinis before dinner to help herself maintain the pretense in which she is engaged.

When she and Anna finally get down to business, it is a parodic situation comparable to the cocktail party. She suggests that they transform Anna's controversial novel about interracial sex into a television musical. Incredulous (this is, after all, 1954), Anna asks, "A musical set in Central Africa?" Without missing a beat, Mrs. Wright replies, "You can be very, very serious in a musical," rebuking Anna to be sure, but only "as a matter of form" (page 292). Needless to say, the interview goes downhill from here, as Anna tries to control her mounting hysteria and Mrs. Wright becomes more obsessed with catching the eye of a fellow diner, a man whom she obviously knows and wishes to spend the night with.

If the sexual dilemma of American women is discussed only by implication in *The Golden Notebook,* it is openly examined in *The Summer Before the Dark* (1973). Here the middle-aged heroine, Kate Brown, an Englishwoman, recognizes in her own behavior the peculiarly American problems related to being available and attractive. Her paradigmatic example is that of the airline hostesses she has observed while visiting the United States. "These girls, dressed fancifully, and in arresting colours, patrol the area alongside the check-in desks of their airline" (6). Their function is not so much to provide "information and guidance," according to Kate, but "to attach the idea of easily available and guiltless sex to that airline" (page 53). In an effort to convey this message, they "smile and smile and smile, and soon it looks as if these girls will one by one float off and up, carried by their own expanding gases of goodwill, which are being constantly replenished by so much attention" (page 53).

Intoxicated by her own attractiveness and the admiring gazes she continually receives from a thousand men a day, each girl becomes hooked on dispensing and receiving love. Once she marries, of course, she can't kick the habit, and the attention of one mere individual is not enough to satisfy her craving. And so, inevitably, she starts to get headaches. "She is frigid and then makes frenetic love to a man who feels as if he had a rival. Soon there is a divorce. Probably she enquires for her old job, but she is too old. She has lost her easy puppy vitality, and her place has been taken by a girl just out of college" (page 55). It doesn't help this poor girl, of course, that her husband is probably another Cy Maitland.

In contrast to her other novels, in *The Four-Gated City* (1969) Lessing is concerned less with Americans' sex lives than with their political influence in the world. There are several references to the McCarthy era and the widespread paranoia it caused. Commenting on the period, the narrator observes that in the United States, "the hysteria had grown till that great nation looked from outside like a dog driven mad by an infestation of fleas, snapping and biting at its own flesh" (7). In this period, "a man called Joe McCarthy, who had no qualities at all, save one, the capacity to terrorize other people, was able to do as he liked" (page 207).

If America seems to be hell-bent on destroying itself from within, it also seems, according to Lessing, at the very least to be indifferent to the possibility that in destroying itself it will destroy the rest of the world. Lessing's concern with this possibility is reflected by the narrator, Martha Quest, who with her friends obsessively collects evidence that the world is indeed gradually going to pieces. Mark Coldridge, for example, sticks on his wall a leaflet advertising the Aldermaston March against nuclear weapons, hanging it next to the 1961 Defense Estimates for the United States, "a figure so enormous that it was meaningless to the ordinary mind" (page 445). In this book the narrator also claims that it was after the height of the Cold War that "Britain's bondage to America . . . was confirmed and built into an economic keystone"; then she adds chauvinistically if accurately that "those years saw Britain's abject role in the arms race laid down" (page 479)—a political resentment and scientific jealousy that is also evident in Fred Hoyle's science fiction masterpiece, *The Black Cloud* (1957).

Later in *The Four-Gated City* Lessing elaborates on Britain's economic bondage to America, when she describes the advent of the "Fascist phase" of British politics (page 590). According to the narrator, this phase, which "had been competently forecast" years ago, is already on the horizon, "ready to come on, gentlemanly, bland, vicious" (page 590). The form she sees it has taken is that of "big business, backed by the landowning Church . . . and Royalty . . . and all taking orders from America" (page 590).

The control America wields over British business interests, and thus over Britain itself, is not "open and straightforward" but perniciously indirect, achieved through the machinations of "international bankers and vaguely named and constituted advisers" (page 590).

The conspiracy the narrator envisions in this passage leads, by novel's end, to the destruction of most of the civilized world. Although the advocates of big business and the defense industries claim it was a series of accidents that destroyed the world, Lessing's narrator clearly believes that the destruction has been intentional, just as Lessing herself clearly believes that the destruction, when it finally does occur in reality, will have been intentionally caused by these interest groups. Whether their intentionality takes the form of malign neglect or purposive action is not entirely clear. What is clear, however, is that as a political writer Doris Lessing is determined to identify what she sees as the very real threat to the future of the world.

That Lessing is a political writer is clear from her fiction and from what she states in her credo, "The Small Personal Voice," in which she demands that literature and its authors be "committed" (8). By this, she hastens to point out, she does not mean that writers should be committed to proselytizing for a particular political party "unless their own private passionate need as writers makes them do so" (page 6). More precisely, what she requires of writers, as apparently she requires of herself, is that they become "instrument[s] of change for good or for bad" (page 6), that they become "architect[s] of the soul" (page 7).

Because she herself has accepted this responsibility of becoming an agent of social change, Lessing takes no pains to camouflage in her fiction either her philosophical or her political opinions. What she stands for is evident in all her writing and can be described as a basic belief in the integrity of the individual and the right of all humans to be themselves. Much like her contemporary, Iris Murdoch, she condemns the temptation to label or pigeonhole people and calls for a genuine respect for the "otherness" of others. At the same time, she also insists that people accept responsibility for themselves and their actions, and not rely on the excuses provided by either religion or psychology. In short, Lessing, like Albert Camus, includes in her concept of individual responsibility the requirement that people be socially responsible, that they show in their actions concern for others. In other words, Lessing's philosophy of personal behavior has political implications for individuals and nations alike (9).

It is, in fact, the political nature of her philosophy that explains why she labels and satirizes Americans. Believing in the essential oneness of life, she is nevertheless not blind to the fact that certain factions are capable of harming others. (No one who has been attending to the events of the twentieth century could be blind to this fact). What frightens Lessing about America and drives her to satirize it is America's very real potential for causing grievous harm to the rest of the world. In other words, it is the great power that America wields, coupled with the inability of its citizens to handle their lives satisfactorily, that so frightens Lessing and finds expression in her extreme anti-American regionalism. She seems to be able to imagine nothing potentially more fatal to the future of the world than having the controls of nuclear weapons in the hands of a nation of neurotics. This is perhaps an apocalyptic explanation of Doris Lessing's anti-American regionalism, but then Doris Lessing is, after all, an apocalyptic writer.

NOTES

1. For studies of the role of Africa in Lessing's fiction, see Michael Thorpe, *Doris Lessing's Africa* (London: Evans Brothers Ltd., 1978), and Mary Ann Singleton, *The*

City and the Veld: The Fiction of Doris Lessing (Lewisburg, Pa: Bucknell University Press, 1977).
2. James Gindin, *Postwar British Fiction: New Accents and Attitudes* (Berkeley and Los Angeles: University of California Press, 1962), 109.
3. Doris Lessing, *Going Home* (New York: Popular Library, 1957, 1968), 51; all page references to this edition.
4. Doris Lessing, *The Golden Natebook* (New York: Bantam Books, 1962, 1973), 51; all page references to this edition.
5. Another example from *The Golden Notebook* is, of course, Saul Green, Anna's American lover, with whom she undergoes a nervous breakdown.
6. Doris Lessing, *The Summer Before the Dark* (New York: Bantam Books, 1973, 1974), 53; all page references to this edition.
7. Doris Lessing, *The Four-Gated City* (New York: Bantam Books, 1969, 1970), 207; all page references to this edition.
8. Doris Lessing, "The Small Personal Voice," in *A Small Personal Voice: Essays, Reviews, Interviews,* ed. Paul Schlueter (New York: Alfred A. Knopf, 1974), 6; all page references to this edition.
9. Lessing's continuing interest in a politically oriented philosophy of personal behavior can be seen in the first four novels of her science fiction series, *Canopus in Argos,* in which she, in one form or another, maintains her conviction that the world is engaged in a self-destructive pattern of activity, marked primarily by selfishness and narrow-mindedness.

SELECT BIBLIOGRAPHY

SPECIALIZED STUDIES

Atwood, Margaret. *Survival: A Thematic Guide to Canadian Literature.* Toronto: Anansi, 1971.

Brown, Dee. *The Gentle Tamers: Women of the Old West.* New York: Bantam, 1958.

Chopin, Kate. *A Kate Chopin Miscellany.* Edited by Per Seyersted, Emily Toth. Oslo, Norway, and Natchitoches, Louisiana: Universitiesforlaget and Northwestern State University Press, 1979.

Cracroft, Richard H., and Neal E. Lambert. *A Believing People: Literature of the Latter-Day Saints.* Provo, UT: Brigham Young Press, 1974.

Davidson, Donald. *The Attack on "Leviathan": Regionalism and Nationalism in the United States.* Chapel Hill, NC: University of North Carolina Press, 1938.

Delsesto, Steven L., and John L. Gilbson, eds. *The Culture of Acadiana: Tradition and Change in South Louisiana.*
Lafayette; LA: University of Southwestern Louisiana, 1975.

Eakin, Paul John. *The New England Girl: Cultural Ideas in Hawthorne, Stowe, Howells, and James.* Athens, GA: University of Georgia Press, 1976.

Elsasser, Nan, Kyle MacKenzie, and Yvonne Tixier y Vigil. *Las Mujeres: Conversations from a Hispanic Community.* Old Westbury, NY, and New York: Feminist Press and McGraw-Hill, 1980.

Fisher, Christiane, ed. *Let Them Speak for Themselves: Women in the American West, 1849–1900.* Hamden, CT: Archon, 1977.

Flanagan, John T., ed. *America Is West: An Anthology of Middlewestern Life and Literature.* Minneapolis: University of Minnesota Press, 1945.

Hampsten, Elizabeth. *Read This Only to Yourself: The Private Writings of Midwestern Women, 1880–1910.* Bloomington, IN: Indiana University Press, 1982.

Hoffmann, Leonore, and Deborah Rosenfelt, eds. *Teaching Women's Literature from a Regional Perspective.* New York: Modern Language Association of America, 1982. (See also *Articles* section, below.)

Jensen, Merrill, ed. *Regionalism in America.* Madison, WI: University of Wisconsin Press, 1951.

Kahn, Kathy, *Hillbilly Women.* Garden City, NY: Doubleday, 1973.

Kolodny, Annette. *The Lay of the Land: Metaphor as Experience and History in American Life and Letters.* Chapel Hill, NC: University of North Carolina Press, 1975.

Lee, Robert Edson. *From West to East: Studies in the Literature of the American West.* Urbana, IL: University of Illinois Press, 1966.

Lerner, Gerda, ed. *Black Women in White America.* New York: Pantheon, 1972.

McWilliams, Carey. *The New Regionalism in American Literature.* Seattle: University of Washington Press, 1930.

Meyer, Roy Willard. *The Middle Western Farm Novel in the Twentieth Century.* Lincoln, NE: University of Nebraska Press, 1965.

Moraga, Cherríe, and Gloria Anzaldua, eds. *This Bridge Called My Back: Writings by Radical Women of Color.* Watertown, MA: Persephone Press, 1981.

Odum, Howard W., and Harry Estill Moore, *American Regionalism: a Cultural-Historical Approach to National Integration.* New York: Henry Holt, 1938.

Post, Lauren C. *Cajun Sketches.* Baton Rouge, LA: Louisiana State University Press, 1962.

Reigelman, Milton M., *The Midland: A Venture in Literary Regionalism.* Iowa City: University of Iowa Press, 1975.
Saxon, Lyle, Robert Tallant, and Edward Dreyer, eds. *Gumbo Ya-Ya.* New York: Bonanza Books, 1945.
Scott, Anne Firor. *The Southern Lady: from Pedestal to Politics, 1830–1930.* Chicago: University of Chicago Press, 1970.
Singleton, Mary Ann. *The City and the Veld: The Fiction of Doris Lessing.* Lewisburg, PA: Bucknell University Press, 1977.
Skaggs, Merrill Maguire. *The Folk of Southern Fiction.* Athens, GA: University of Georgia Press, 1972.
Stegner, Wallace. *The Sound of Mountain Water: the Changing American West.* Garden City, NY: Doubleday, 1969.
Stewart, Elinore Pruitt. *Letters of a Woman Homesteader.* Lincoln, NE: University of Nebraska Press, 1961.
Stewart, Randall. *Regionalism and Beyond.* Nashville, TN: Vanderbilt University Press, 1968.
Thomas, Clara. *The Manawaka World of Margaret Laurence.* Toronto: McClelland and Stewart, 1976.
Thorpe, Michael. *Doris Lessing's Africa.* London: Evans Brothers Ltd., 1978.
Twelve Southerners. *I'll Take My Stand: the South and the Agrarian Tradition.* New York: Harper and Brothers, 1930.
Walker, Margaret. *How I Wrote Jubilee.* Chicago: Third World, 1972.
West, Ray B., Jr. *Writing in the Rocky Mountains.* Lincoln, NE: University of Nebraska Press, 1947.
Westbrook, Perry. *Acres of Flint: Writers of Rural New England, 1870–1900.* Washington, DC: Scarecrow Press, 1951.

GENERAL WORKS

Auerbach, Nina. *Communities of Women: an Idea in Fiction.* Cambridge, MA: Harvard University Press, 1978.
Cott, Nancy F. *The Bonds of Womanhood.* New Haven, CT: Yale University Press, 1977.
———, ed. *Root of Bitterness.* New York: Dutton, 1972.
Davidson, Cathy N., and E. M. Broner. *The Lost Tradition:*

Mothers and Daughters in Literature. New York: Frederick Ungar, 1980.

Delaney, Janice, Mary Jane Lupton, and Emily Toth. *The Curse: A Cultural History of Menstruation.* New York: Dutton, 1976.

Diamond, Arlyn, and Lee R. Edwards, eds. *The Authority of Experience: Essays in Feminist Criticism.* Amherst; MA: University of Massachusetts Press, 1977.

Edwards, Lee R., and Arlyn Diamond, eds. *American Voices, American Women.* New York: Avon, 1973.

Fisher, Dexter, ed. *The Third Woman: Minority Women Writers of the United States.* Boston: Houghton Mifflin, 1980.

Hull, Gloria T., Patricia Bell Scott, and Barbara Smith, eds. *But Some of Us Are Brave: Black Women's Studies.* New York: The Feminist Press, 1982.

Koppelman Cornillon, Susan. *Images of Women in Fiction: Feminist Perspectives.* Bowling Green, OH: Popular Press, 1972.

Lerner, Gerda. *The Female Experience: an American Documentary.* Indianapolis: Bobbs-Merrill, 1977.

Merriam, Eve. *Growing Up Female in America: Ten Lives.* Garden City, NY: Doubleday, 1971.

Moffat, Mary Jane, and Charlotte Painter, eds. *Revelations: Diaries of Women.* New York: Vintage, 1975.

Olsen, Tillie, *Silences.* New York: Delacorte, 1978.

Toth, Emily. *Inside Peyton Place: the Life of Grace Metalious.* New York: Doubleday, 1981.

Welter, Barbara. *Dimity Convictions: the American Woman in the Nineteenth Century.* Athens: Ohio Unversity Press, 1976.

ARTICLES

(*TWL=Teaching Women's Literature from a Regional Perspective,* edited by Leonore Hoffmann and Deborah Rosenfelt. New York: Modern Language Association of America, 1982. This volume also has an extensive bibliography.)

Angell, Susan, Jacquelyn D. Hall, Candace Waid, eds. "Genera-

tions: Women in the South." Special Issue of *Southern Exposure* 4 (Winter 1977).
Armitage, Susan H. "'Aunt Amelia's Diary': The Record of a Reluctant Pioneer." *TWL*, 69–73.
Austin, Mary. "Regionalism in American Fiction." *English Journal* 21 (February 1932): 97–106.
Bader, Julia. "The 'Rooted' Landscape and the Woman Writer." *TWL*, 23–30.
Baker, Joseph E. "Four Arguments for Regionalism." *Saturday Review of Literature* 15 (28 November 1936): 3–4, 14.
Beath, Paul Robert. "The Fallacies of Regionalism." *Saturday Review of Literature* 15 (28 November 1936): 3–4, 14, 16.
Bolsterli, Margaret Jones. "On the Literary Uses of Private Documents." *TWL*, 44–54.
"The Boom in Regionalism." *Saturday Review of Literature* 10 (7 April 1934): 606.
Brett, Sally Alexander. "The Editor and the Writer: An Approach to Archival Manuscripts." *TWL*, 132–139.
Bullock, Florence Haxton. "Kentucky Hill Folk, Vividly Seen." *New York Herald Tribune Books*, 25 June 1949, 5
Cantarow, Ellen. "Sex, Race, and Criticism: Thoughts of a White Feminist on Kate Chopin and Zora Neale Hurston." *Radical Teacher* 9 (1978): 30–33.
Carver, Ann Cathey. "From Concept to Classroom." *TWL*, 105–117.
Culley, Margo. "Feminist Pedagogy: Lost Voices of American Women." *TWL*, 84–91.
———. "Hints for Evaluating 'Literary Qualities in Nontraditional Materials." *TWL*, 188.
Culley, Margo, and Adele Friedman. "Public Presentation Reports." *TWL*, 158–162.
Davidson, Donald. "Regionalism and Nationalism in American Literature." *American Review* 5 (April 1935): 48–61.
Davis, Barbara Hillyer. "New Forms for New Research." *TWL*, 163–171.
Donovan, Josephine, *New England and Local Color: A Study of Women's Literary Realism,* NY: Ungar, 1983.
Faragher, Johnny, and Christine Stansell. "Women and Their

Families on the Overland Trail to California and Oregon, 1842–1867." *Feminist Studies* 2 (1975): 150–166.

"Focus on Women Writers." Special Issue of *Georgia Review* 33 (Winter 1979).

Franklin, Phyllis. "Faulkner, Arnow and the 1955 National Book Award." *Resources in Education* 13:7 (July 1978): 54.

Geary, Edward A. "Mormondom's Lost Generation: The Novelists of the 1940s." *Brigham Young University Studies* 18 (Fall 1977): 89–98.

———. "The Poetics of Provincialism: Mormon Regional Fiction." *Dialogue: a Journal of Mormon Thought* 11:2 (Summer 1978): 15–24.

Gladney, Rose, Alice A. Parker, and Elizabeth A. Meese. "Southern Women's Literature and Culture: Course Development and the Pedagogical Process." *TWL*, 118–131.

Goodman, Charlotte. "Images of American Rural Women in the Novel." *University of Michigan Papers in Women's Studies* 1 (June 1975): 54–71.

Grevatt, Marge. "Dusting the Mirror: Reseaching Women's History." *TWL*, 74–83.

———. "Oral History as a Resource in Teaching Women's Studies." *TWL*, 150–157.

Hampsten, Elizabeth. "Tell Me All You Know: Reading Letters and Diaries of Rural Women." *TWL*, 55–63.

Hobbs, Glenda. "A Portrait of the Artist as Mother: Harriette Arnow and *The Dollmaker*." *Georgia Review* 33 (Winter 1979): 851–867.

Hull, Gloria T. "Alice Dunbar-Nelson: A Regional Approach." *TWL*, 64–68.

———. "Rewriting Afro-American Literature: a Case for Black Women Writers." *Radical Teacher* 6 (December 1977): 10–14.

Jones, Anne Goodwyn. *Tomorrow Is Another Day: The Woman Writer in the South*. Baton Rouge: Louisiana State University Press, 1980.

Jones, Douglas. "Civilization and Geologic Consent: Region from a Geologist's Perspective." *TWL*, 208–213.

Jorgensen, Bruce W. "'Herself Moving Beside Herself, Out There Alone': The Shape of Mormon Belief in Virginia

Sorensen's *The Evening and the Morning.*" *Dialogue: A Journal of Mormon Thought* 13:3 (Fall 1980): 43–60.

McLeod, Norman, *et al.* "Regionalism: A Symposium." *Sewance Review* 39 (October-December 1931): 456–483.

Maglin, Nan Bauer. "Full of Memories': Teaching Matrilineage." *TWL*, 92–104.

Meese, Elizabeth. "The Whole Truth: Frameworks for the Study of Women's Noncanonical Literature." *TWL*, 15–22.

Parker, Alice A. "Cross-Cultural Perspectives: Creole and Acadian Women." *TWL*, 31–43.

Patterson-Black, Sheryll. "Women Homesteaders of the Great Plains." *Frontiers: a Journal of Women Studies* 1 (Spring 1976): 67–88.

Ransom, John Crowe. "The Aesthetics of Regionalism." *American Review* 2 (January 1934): 290–310.

"Regionalism or the Coterie Manifesto." *Saturday Review of Literature* 15 (28 November 1936), 8.

Register, Cheri. "American Feminist Literary Criticism: A Bibliographical Introduction," in *Feminist Literary Criticism: Explorations in Theory*. Edited by Josephine Donovan. (Lexington, KY: University Press of Kentucky, 1975), 1–28.

Ricou, Laurence R. "Empty as Nightmare: Man and Landscape in Recent Canadian Prairie Fiction." *Mosaic* 6:2 (1973): 143—160.

Rushing, Jane Gilmore. "The Roots of a Novel." *The Writer* 88:7 (July 1975): 9–11, 46.

Saxton, Ruth O. "Letters and Diaries: Demystifying Archival Research for Undergraduates." *TWL*, 140–149.

Showalter, Elaine. "Review Essay: Literary Criticism." *Signs* 1 (Winter 1975): 435–460.

Sillitoe, Linda. "The Upstream Swimmers: Female Rebels as Protagonists in Mormon Novels." *Sunstone* 4:5 (1979): 52.

Smith, Barbara. "Doing Research on Black Women." *Radical Teacher* 6 (December 1977): 25–27.

———. "Toward a Black Feminist Criticism." *But Some of Us Are Brave: Black Women's Studies,* eds. Gloria T. Hull, Patricia Bell Scott, and Barbara Smith. NY: Feminist Press, 1982, 157–175.

Smith-Rosenberg, Carroll. "The Female World of Love and Ritual: Relations Between Women in Nineteenth-Century America." *Signs* 1:1 (Autumn 1975): 1–29.

———. "The New Woman and the New History." *Feminist Studies* 3 (Fall 1975): 185–198.

Stitzel, Judith, "Authentic Voices." *TWL*, 172–175.

Tate, Allen. "Regionalism and Sectionalism." *New Republic* 69 (23 December 1931): 158–159.

Toth, Emily. "Regionalism: A Dirty Word?" *North Dakota English* 2 (July 1977): 5–11.

Walker, Alice. "In Search of Our Mothers' Gardens." *Ms.*, May 1974, 64–70.

Warren, Robert Penn. "Not Local Color." *Virginia Quarterly Review* 8:1 (1932): 153–160.

———. "Some Don'ts for Literary Regionalists." *American Review* 8 (December 1936): 142–150.

Welty, Eudora. "Place in Fiction," in *Three Papers on Fiction*. (Northampton, MA: Smith College, 1962), 1–15.

Wood, Ann Douglas. "The Literature of Impoverishment: The Women Local Colorists in America, 1865–1914." *Women's Studies* 1 (1972): 3–40.

Zak, Michele W. "*The Grass Is Singing:* a Little Novel about the Emotions." *Contemporary Literature* 14 (Autumn 1973): 481–490. Reprinted in *Doris Lessing: Critical Studies*. Edited by Annis Pratt and L. S. Dembo (Madison, WI: University of Wisconsin, 1974), 64–74.

NOTES ON CONTRIBUTORS

ARNOLD E. DAVIDSON, professor of English at Michigan State University, has published some 50 articles, mostly on modern literature. His book on Mordecai Richler (Ungar) is in press, and he is currently completing a book on Jean Rhys. With Cathy N. Davidson, he co-edited *The Art of Margaret Atwood* (Anansi of Toronto, 1981).

CATHY N. DAVIDSON, associate professor of English at Michigan State University, has published dozens of essays and reviews on North American literature in periodicals such as *American Literature, Canadian Literature,* and *Ms.* She has edited three collections of scholarly essays, including (with E. M. Broner), *The Lost Tradition: Mothers and Daughters in Literature* (Ungar, 1980).

KATHERINE FISHBURN is associate professor of English at Michigan State University, where she teaches courses in women's, Commonwealth, and contemporary literature. She is the author of *Women in Popular Culture* (Greenwood Press, 1982) and *Richard Wright's Hero* (Scarecrow Press, 1977).

EDWARD A. GEARY is professor of English and graduate coordinator at Brigham Young University. He has published articles on Henry James and Joseph Conrad as well as regional topics.

CHARLOTTE GOODMAN, associate professor of English at Skidmore College, has published articles on Joyce Carol Oates, William Faulkner, Henry James, and Tillie Olsen, among others. She is currently working on a study of Jean Stafford and on doubling in works by and abut women. Her Afterword to the Feminist Press edition of Edith Summers Kelley's *Weeds* was published in 1982.

GLENDA HOBBS has taught literature and writing at Boston College, then worked in script development at the Mark Taper Forum, a regional theater in Los Angeles. She is now a playwright and apprentice stage director at the American Repertory Theater in Cambridge, Mass. Her articles on Sarah Orne Jewett and Harriette Arnow have appeared in *Studies in Short Fiction, Georgia Review*, and the *Dictionary of Literary Biography*. Her most recent essay, on Harriette Arnow's early career, appears on *Literature at the Barricades: The American Writer in the 1930s* (University of Alabama Press, 1982). She has also written an adaptation of Sarah Orne Jewett's *Country of the Pointed Firs* for WGBH radio, Boston.

BARBARA A. JOHNS is assistant professor of English at Marygrove College in Detroit. She is currently at work on a study of the spinster in the works of New England women regionalists (Rose Terry Cooke, Harriet Beecher Stowe, Mary E. Wilkins Freeman, Sarah Orne Jewett).

BERNARD J. KOLOSKI is professor of English at Mansfield University in Pennsylvania; from 1981 to 1984 he was Fulbright Professor of American Literature at the University of Silesia in Poland. He has published essays on Kate Chopin, bibliotherapy, and guidelines for the use of tutors in college developmental programs. He is continuing work on both Kate Chopin and Edith Gleckler.

NOTES ON CONTRIBUTORS

PAUL SOLYN is director of foundation and corporate support at Oberlin College. His collection of poems, *Mistress Quickly's Garden,* was published by Raintree Press in 1978.

EMILY TOTH, associate professor of English and American studies at Pennsylvania State University, is co-author of *The Curse: A Cultural History of Menstruation* (with Janice Delaney and Mary Jane Lupton; Dutton, 1976, and New American Library, 1977). She is also assistant editor of *A Kate Chopin Miscellany* (with Per Seyersted; Oslo and Natchitoches: Universitetsforlaget and Northwestern State University of Louisiana, 1979). Her most recent publications are a biography, *Inside Peyton Place: The Life of Grace Metalious* (Doubleday, 1981), and a historical novel, *Daughters of New Orleans* (Bantam, 1983). She is now writing a new biography of Kate Chopin, under contract to Atheneum.

SUSAN ALLEN TOTH, professor of English at Macalester College, is the author of *Blooming: A Small-Town Girlhood* (Little, Brown, 1981; paperback, 1982). Her fiction and essays have appeared in *Ms, Harper's,* and *Redbook,* as well as in *American Literature, Studies in Short Fiction, New England Quarterly,* and others. (Susan Allen Toth and Emily Toth are not related.)

ROGER WHITLOW, professor of English at Eastern Illinois University, is the author of more than 40 articles. He has published three books: *Black American Literature* (Nelson-Hall, 1973), *The Darker Vision* (Gordon Press, 1977), and *Many Yankee Faces* (Gordon Press, 1979).

INDEX

Anti-American regionalism, 177–187
Anzaldua, Gloria, 11
Appalachia, 84
Arnow, Harriette, 83–90
Austin, Mary, 88

Barren Ground (Glasgow), 96
Berthoff, Warner, 25
Bird in the House (Laurence), 135, 137
Bishop, John Peale, 150
Blithedale Romance (Hawthorne), 30, 51
Bly, Robert, 72
"Boston marriage," 21
Bostonians, The (James), 30, 34, 41, 47
Brooks, Gwendolyn, 70, 76
Brown, Alice, 16, 17, 18, 24–25
Bruccoli, Matthew, 93, 94
Butterfly Ward, The (Gilboord), 168, 173, 175

Cable, George Washington, 109, 118–119
Canada, in regional novel, 129–135, 168
Cather, Willa, 167
Children of God (Fisher), 140
Chopin, Kate, 10, 87, 109, 155
Cooke, Rose Terry, 16, 17, 18, 21–23
Country of the Pointed Firs, The (Jewett), 17, 20, 25, 30
Country People (Suckow), 96

Creoles, 118–121

Davidson, Donald, 88
Devil's Hand, The (Kelley), 93, 94, 95
DeVoto, Bernard, 140
Diviners, The (Laurence), 135, 136
Divorce, 22–23
Dollmaker, The (Arnow), 83, 84, 86
Dunbar, Paul Laurence, 109, 116–117, 118
Dunbar-Nelson, Alice, 109–124

Elsie Venner (Holmes), 30, 51
Ethan Frome (Wharton), 30, 57
Etter, Dave, 78
Evening and the Morning, The (Sorensen), 146

Fear of Flying (Jong), 16
Feminism, 10, 29, 32
Fetterly, Judith, 49
Fire-Dwellers, The (Laurence), 133–134
Fisher, Dexter, 11
Fisher, Vardis, 140
Ford, Ford Madox, 150
Four-Gated City, The (Lessing), 184–186
Freeman, Mary E. Wilkins, 16, 17, 18–21, 23–24, 87
   spinsters in works by, 33, 34–36, 38, 43

Gentle Americans, The (Howe), 21
Giant Joshua, The (Whipple), 141, 147–149
Gilboord, Margaret Gibson, 167–175
Girl on a White Gate (Siporin), 76–77
Glasgow, Ellen, 96
Gleckler, Edith, 156–164
Going Home (Lessing), 179–180
Golden Notebook, The (Lessing), 180–183
Goodness of St. Rocque and Other Stories, The (Dunbar), 109, 113, 118
Gross, Barry, 71

Hawthorne, Nathaniel, 31, 32, 36, 51, 58–59
Holmes, Oliver Wendell, 53
Home, 9–10
House of the Seven Gables, The (Hawthorne), 30, 45
Howe, Helen, 21
Howells, William Dean, 33, 36, 37
Hunter's Horn (Arnow), 84, 85–86

James, Henry, 34, 40–41
Jest of God, A (Laurence), 129–133
Jewett, Sarah Orne, 16, 17, 18, 20, 24–26, 87, 167
  spinsters in works by, 34, 38, 39
Jilted-woman theme, 112–113
Jong, Erica, 15

Kane, Harnett T., 86
Kate Chopin Newsletter, The, 10, 11
Kazin, Alfred, 85
Kelley, Edith Summers, 93–104
Kelley, Fred, 95
Kentucky, in regional writing, 83, 84, 85, 87, 89
Krutch, Joseph Wood, 94

Late George Apley, The (Marquand), 30, 55
Laurence, Margaret, 129–137

Lessing, Doris, 177–187
Lewis, Sinclair, 93–94
Liberty Valley (Pennsylvania), 157–159, 163
Local color
  as literary movement, 83, 87
  in New England writing, 16–18, 22–23, 26
  in north-central Pennsylvania, 157–159
Loggins, Vernon, 116, 118

"Making It" (Gilboord), 168–173
Manawaka, Manitoba, 129–130, 132–133, 134, 135
Many Heavens (Sorensen), 147
Marriage, 22–23, 24, 26
Masterpieces of Negro Eloquence (Dunbar-Nelson), 110
Masters, Edgar Lee, 73
McGrath, Thomas, 71, 78
Metcalf, Eugene, 109, 110
Midwest
  cities of, 74, 75
  definition of, 67–68
  literary tradition of, 71
  poetry of, 68–78
Moore, Alice Ruth; *see* Dunbar-Nelson, Alice
Moraga, Cherrie, 11
Mormon Country
  definition of, 139
  and regional writing, 140
  settlement of, 142–143
Mormon Country (Stegner), 144
Mountain Path (Arnow), 84–85
Mourning Becomes Electra (O'Neill), 30, 50
"Mr. Baptiste" (Dunbar-Nelson), 121–122
Mueller, Lisel, 68–78
Murdoch, Iris, 186–187

Need to Hold Still, The (Mueller), 77
Nelson, Robert J., 109

New England
   local color writing in, 16–18, 22–23, 26
   spinsterhood in, 30
New Orleans, and regional writing, 109, 110, 121

Oldtown Folks (Stowe), 16, 17
Outrageous, 168

Peabody, Elizabeth, 32
People of Color in Louisiana (Dunbar-Nelson), 110
Private Life, The (Mueller), 68

RATFI; *see* Regionalism and the Female Imagination
Rebirth of Jacob Winningstadt, The (Gleckler), 155, 156–163
Regionalism and the Female Imagination (journal), 10, 11
Revolt of Mother and Other Stories, The (Freeman), 30
Rise of Silas Lapham, The (Howells), 30
Roberts, Elizabeth Maddox, 96
Robinson, Edward Arlington, 73, 74
Roethke, Theodore, 78
Russell, Craig, 169

Sandburg, Carl, 71
Scarlet Letter, The (Hawthorne), 30–33
Sherwood, Mary E. Wilson, 16–17
Single life, 22–24, 25–26; *see also* Spinsterhood
Siporin, Ona, 76–77
Sorensen, Virginia, 140, 141–142, 144–145, 146–147, 150
Sound of Mountain Water, The (Stegner), 143
Spinsterhood, in New England regional writing, 29–59; *see also* Single life
Stafford, William, 74, 78
Stegner, Wallace, 141, 143–144
Stone Angel, The (Laurence), 133
Stowe, Harriet Beecher, 16, 42
Suckow, Ruth, 96
Summer Before the Dark, The (Lessing), 184

Tate, Allen, 89–90
Third Woman, The (Fisher), 11
This Bridge Called My Back (Moraga and Anzaldua), 11
Time of Man, The (Roberts), 96
"Tony's Wife" (Dunbar-Nelson), 122–124

Uncle Tom's Cabin (Stowe), 30, 34
Updegraff, Allan, 94, 95

Violets and Other Tales (Moore), 109, 110–112, 116

Wagoner, David, 75–76
Warren, Robert Penn, 88
Waugh, Alec, 150
Weeds (Kelley), 93, 94, 95, 96–104
Wells, Kate Gannett, 16
Whipple, Maurine, 140, 141, 146, 147–150
Williams, William Carlos, 72
Wright, James, 74, 78

Young, Brigham, 140, 143, 149–150

INDEX OF FICTIONAL CHARACTERS

Alexander, Kate, 146–147
Apley, Catharine, 55–57
Apley, George, 55–57
Ashley, Brett, 26

Birdseye, Miss, 34, 40–41, 43, 47
Britton, Louisa, 33, 34–35, 43, 53

Cameron, Rachel, 130–134
Chancellor, Olive, 41, 47–50, 51, 54, 57

Darley, Helen, 53–55
Dent, Miss Temperance, 39, 43, 47

Ellis, Louisa, 43–45, 46, 55, 56

Fairweather, Eunice, 33, 34–35, 53
Frome, Ethan, 57–58
Frome, Zeena, 57–58

Gunn, Morag, 136–137

Lapham, Irene, 36–37, 38, 46
Lapham, Penelope, 33, 36, 37

MacAindra, Stacey Cameron, 133–134
MacLeod, Vanessa, 135

Mannon, Lavinia, 50–51, 57
McIntyre, Clory, 148–149
Moore, Inez, 33, 34–35, 43

Pippinger, Judith, 96–104
Prance, Dr. Mary, 34, 39, 41–42, 43, 47
Priscilla *(Blithedale Romance)*, 51–53, 54
Prynne, Hester, 30–33, 35, 36, 38, 43, 47, 51, 55
Pyncheon, Hepzibah, 45–47, 48

Ransom, Basil, 41, 48, 49, 54

St. Clare, Ophelia, 39, 42–43
Shipley, Hagar, 133
Sophie, Miss, 113–114

Tarrant, Verena, 48–50
Titee, 115–116
Todd, Joanna, 34, 36, 38–39, 47, 48, 51

Venner, Elsie, 53–54

Winningstadt, Jacob, 159–163
Winningstadt, Jennie, 160–163
Wulf, Anna (Ella), 180–183

7934